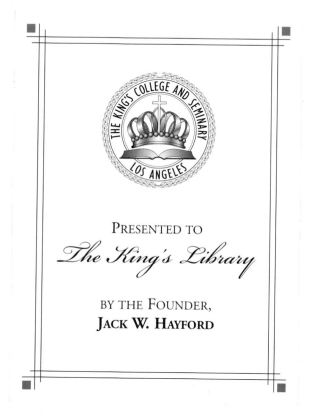

SPECIAL EDITION

This copy of this special edition of

IT'S IN THE BIBLE

is being presented with love and appreciation
from the author.

I am praying that as you read the words of this book, it might help you get a fresh and exciting view of the real character of God. I am praying that if you have added to or taken away from the characteristics of God, that all of that distortion will be eliminated and you will come to know God in a better way. To know Him is to love Him.

May God bless you with happiness and loving friends and relatives. May He bless you with a quiet peace in your soul. May He bless you with a real love for Him and for your fellow man. May you be the recipient of oceans of love. May He bless you and take care of all your financial needs. May He bless you with health and vigor of body and soul. May He bless you with security and may your security primarily be found in Him. May He bless you with a long life, full of outstanding opportunities. May He show His mercy and compassion to you throughout all of your days.

Love in Christ,

James McKeever, Ph.D., Th.D.

A needed book! The idea of presenting the other side of God in order to understand His complete nature is valid.

—Jim Burck
Pastor, Texas

I feel that this book is very important and perhaps one of the best you have ever written. There is considerable meat in it.

—Roger Minor
Attorney, California

It will be great for developing maturity and understanding of real truth among Christians. I certainly agree with the content.

—Doug Clark
Evangelist, Washington

As I went through the manuscript you sent me, I was impressed by your subjects and the way in which you presented them. I feel that you presented each subject with a careful, objective approach. . . . It was stimulating to me.

—Charlie Cutts
Pastor, Wisconsin

I must tell you that when I came to the last section—your masterful defense of the resurrection—I closed the book shouting HALLELUJAH to Jesus! Regardless of the rest, this section needs to be published for the benefit of the great lay readership in the church today! There is nothing quite like it as far as I know.

—Dr. F. Carlton Booth,
Treasurer, World Vision

Believe It or Not . . .

IT'S IN THE BIBLE

by

DR. JAMES McKEEVER

Unless otherwise indicated, all Scripture quotations are taken from the *New American Standard Bible*, Copyright © The Lockman Foundation 1960, 1962, 1963, 1968, 1971, 1973, 1975, 1977. Used by permission.

Scripture quotations identified **KJV** are from the *King James Version* of the Bible. Scripture quotations identified NKJV are from the *New King James Version*, Copyright © Thomas Nelson, Inc. 1979, 1980, 1982. Scripture quotations identified **Amplified** are taken from *The Amplified Bible*, Copyright © Zondervan Publishing House 1965, 1979. Used by permission.

IT'S IN THE BIBLE

Copyright © 1988 by James M. McKeever

Printed in the United States of America
First printing June, 1988

Omega Publications
P. O. Box 4130
Medford, Oregon 97501 (U.S.A.)

ISBN #0-86694-109-6 (Hardback)

TABLE OF CONTENTS

This book is dedicated first and foremost
to the glory of God
and His only begotten Son,
Jesus Christ,
with special thanks to the Holy Spirit
for His teaching, guidance and insights.

On the human level,
this book is dedicated to all believers
of all nations
who are seeking the truth of God,
to know the real God of the Bible,
and who are willing to put aside
their personal prejudices
based on their culture,
in order to go back and find out
what God is truly like,
as depicted in the pages of the Bible.

It is also dedicated to every member
of the Omega staff,
the Omega Family and the Omega Team,
whose prayers and support
made this book possible.

A special dedication is made
to two couples who have stood by us
in a very special way:

Jack and Mary Hoskins
Dave and Jackie Cunningham

INTRODUCTION

The Lord has led me to write several books. In most cases, I understood why I was writing the book before I began. *The Aids Plague* was obviously being written to help people understand what was happening in the world with regard to this dreaded disease, and to help them to protect themselves and their communities. *Financial Guidance* was written to help Christians bring their financial concerns into an order that would reflect good stewardship and be pleasing to the Lord. *Revelation for Laymen* was designed to help the average individual understand the exciting conclusion of the Bible. And so it was with all of the other books that I have written.

However, with *It's in the Bible*, it was different. I felt the Lord wanted me to write it, but I had no idea why—until I got to the last chapter of the book. Then it became clear to me that the reason the Lord wanted me to write this book was to help people see the true character of God and to point out some of the characteristics that we have falsely attributed to God. In reality, many of us are worshiping a God whom we have modified to fit our own concepts.

Once I realized what the purpose of the book was, I went back and added to the various chapters, so that each of them would bring out this underlying theme. Of course, I have not even attempted to express the complete character of God, but I have tried to present some scriptural insights that will help the reader develop a clearer picture of who God really is and the true nature of His character.

One of the reasons that a more accurate and complete understanding of God's character is so important is this. During the end of this age, God may ask various ones of us to do things that may seem unusual to us. If our image of God is such that we are led to believe that God would never ask us to do these unusual things, we are likely to fail to obey God's call. I believe it is absolutely essential to have the most accurate picture possible of the true character of God, so that when He asks something of us we will not disregard His request, because it conflicts with a false belief we may have about God's character.

In your daily Bible reading, I would encourage you to keep your spirit and your eyes alert to clues as to what the true God of the Bible is really like. As you do that, you will come to know Him better, and to know Him better is to love Him more.

You may find some things in this book—and in the Bible—that may startle you, at first. However, I would ask you to prayerfully continue with the book, to see how all things fit together perfectly in God's overall plan and to come to know more about God's overall character.

The translation of the Bible primarily used in this book is the *New American Standard* (NAS). This is the translation that Dr. Walter Martin, the "Bible Answer Man," recommends. The reason that he and I prefer it is that, as scholars agree, it is the closest to a literal translation of the Greek and Hebrew.

I would encourage you to breathe a little prayer, asking the Holy Spirit to speak to you through this book, that He might draw you closer to the real God of the Bible.

—James McKeever

ACKNOWLEDGEMENTS

Of course, the first and foremost acknowledgement must be to our Father God, who placed the concept of this book on my heart; to the Holy Spirit who gave me inspiration; and to Jesus Christ, my Lord and Savior. With my whole heart, I want only to glorify God in this book, and in everything that I do in life.

On the human level, I am greatly indebted to my assistant, Jackie Cunningham, who faithfully typed the book and labored shoulder-to-shoulder with me during its writing and preparation. I am equally indebted to my precious brother in Christ, Jim Andrews, who helped with the editing, did the technical work with the computers and the typesetting, and made valuable suggestions.

However, top billing must go to my precious wife, Jeani, who has spent more time on this book than I have. The quality of this book is the result of her careful and conscientious editing. However, she was not just the editor—she really would qualify to be the co-author. Many of the chapter conclusions she wrote entirely, as well as other major passages. Her constructive criticism and suggestions of Scriptures to include helped round out the book, making it as full and complete as possible. Not only did we work together in this way, but she also gave constant, cheerful encouragement and the tender love that only a wonderful, caring wife can give. Without her, this book would most likely not exist.

I am also indebted to the men of God who read through the rough manuscript and gave me both encouraging comments and very valuable criticisms. Acknowledging them here does not mean that they agree with everything that is in this book. I love them deeply and appreciate them taking the time to read the manuscript and to give me their comments.

I never want to go off on some wild tangent, as sometimes happens to authors, even Christian ones. As protection from this pitfall, I always submit new manuscripts to men of God who will help me avoid error. The men who read through this manuscript and provided much helpful feedback are:

Carlton Booth	Jack Hoskins
Jim Burck	Gary Matsdorf
Giff Claiborne	Roger Minor
Doug Clark	Mike Vessey
Charlie Cutts	Ed Gruman

I also want to express my love and appreciation to the Omega Family, the Omega Team and others who receive our monthly publication, *End-Times News Digest*, who have prayed faithfully with us as this book was being developed. Great things are wrought by prayer, and their prayers have been a protection for this book from the attacks of the evil one. They have also held up my hands when I was weary in writing. I want to personally thank each and every one of them, and pray God's richest blessings upon them.

My last acknowledgement and word of appreciation goes to you, the reader, for a book would be valueless, if no one read or benefitted from it. I am really praying that the Holy Spirit will cause you to recognize the things in this book that are truth from God. I am also praying that, if I have missed the mark in any area, and there is anything in this book that is not the absolute truth of God, the Holy Spirit will simply eradicate it from your mind and cause you not even to remember it. My purpose is to help you develop a clearer picture of some things in the Bible that are often ignored and, hopefully, to acquire a clearer picture of God, His character and your relationship to Him.

Please pray with me for the Christians who will misunderstand this book. I believe God is calling us to a new holiness and righteousness, but it must conform to His definition, not that of man or man's culture and traditions. I am not advocating a libertine or hedonistic life. I am advocating a life dedicated to God.

My thanks to everyone who had a part in making this book a reality.

—James McKeever

PREFACE

Since the first time James mentioned the concept of this book, I have seen the valuable role that such a book could play. So many of us allow our image of God to be formed by bits and pieces of what we have heard others say, instead of going to the Bible itself to see what it has to say about who God really is. He loves us so much and desires that we have an intimate, loving relationship with Him. He wants us to spend time getting to know Him, and one valuable way to do so is to read about Him in the Bible. So much of His character is revealed there.

I expect that *It's in the Bible* will challenge many Christians to delve deeper into the Scriptures to find things that perhaps they have missed in the past, and that is good. I also see many who don't profess to be Christians being intrigued to learn what colorful stories the Bible contains. If this book serves to help all of us spend more time reading and studying the Bible, God certainly *can* and will reveal Himself, His true character and His truth for our lives, as we read its pages.

—Jeani McKeever

1

IT AIN'T NECESSARILY SO

There are many things that many Christian leaders and teachers wish were not in the Bible. There are things in the Bible that are absolutely shocking. An incredible number of things that people believe are in the Bible are not. Let's look at a few of these.

SHOCKING THINGS IN THE BIBLE

There are a number of things in the Bible, even in our English translations, that would shock most people, if they ever read them. If you go back to the original languages, the shock is even greater. For example, did you know that:

1. God told one of His prophets to marry a hooker? Then, after she left him and went back to hooking, He told him to go get her and marry her again?
2. God told one of His prophets to go absolutely naked for three years?
3. One of the kings of Israel had to give a hundred foreskins from the penises of Philistines as a dowry in order to get married?

4. The heads of four of the tribes of Israel were not born from Leah or Rachel, but from Jacob's mistresses?

5. You are told that you can, under certain circumstances, take your tithe and go out and buy wine and strong drink with it?

6. Almost all of the Old Testament saints had multiple wives and multiple mistresses?

7. The Bible clearly says there are sea monsters and dragons?

THINGS THAT ARE NOT IN THE BIBLE

Many people believe that certain things are in the Bible which are not. For example, did you know that:

1. No place does the Bible say that there were three wise men?

2. The wise men did not come to the stable where Christ was born, but went to the "house" where He was staying when He was about two years old?

3. The angels, when they appeared to the shepherds, did not sing?

4. Jesus is never called "The Rose of Sharon" in the Bible?

5. Jesus is never called "The Lily of the Valley" in the Bible?

6. The Bible never says that "the lion will lie down with the lamb"?

7. The Bible does not say, "God helps those who help themselves"?

8. The Bible does not say that all prayers are answered or even heard by God?

9. Christianity totally stands or falls based on whether or not Christ was raised from the dead?

10.   The Bible does not forbid the drinking of wine for the populace?

These are but a few of the host of things that people think are in the Bible which in fact are not. We will examine most of these later in this book.

WE MUST TAKE THE BIBLE AS IT IS

There are things that many people wish were not in the Bible. There are things that some leaders may even try to hide from their people, things that clearly are in the Bible. In fact, I was discussing this book with Ann Murchison, wife of the late, great Clint Murchison, former owner of the Dallas Cowboys. She travels extensively teaching the Bible. In response, she said, "There are many things that are in the Bible that *I* don't want anyone to know anything about!" This is not atypical among even outstanding Bible teachers of our day.

This book goes "all the way" and brings to light many things that are in the Bible that teachers would just as soon ignore. It may be shocking to many Christians and Jews to discover some of these things in the Bible that are totally unknown to them. Some atheists and agnostics may use it as ammunition for questioning their religious friends. My hope and my prayer is that it will force people, regardless of their beliefs, to go back to the Bible and search out these and other things for themselves.

You may hate this book; you may love this book, but you will not read through it with neutral emotions, because all of the things in here—believe it or not—*are* in the Bible.

Just a personal note, lest anyone accuse me of advocating immoral living, I am not promoting anything of the sort. I am simply revealing what the Bible has to say; people can then do with it as they wish. Your argument, if you develop one, is with the Bible and God, not with me. I am just a messenger bringing these subjects to light.

MY FAVORITE BOOK

The Bible has been my favorite book since 1938. I have spent many thousands of hours reading it, studying it, and pondering it. Through the years, I kept running across unusual and sometimes strange things. I keep a journal of things the Lord teaches me, and other interesting subjects, and have done so for many years. I am excited to share with you a few of the things that I have discovered in the fifty years that I have been studying the Bible.

THE BEST-SELLING BOOK,
BUT THE LEAST READ

The Bible is by far the best-selling book in the world, and has been for centuries. However, simultaneously it is probably also the least read book in the world. People buy Bibles to give away as Christmas presents, graduation presents, birthday presents and presents for other occasions. However, by and large, the recipients leave them in their bookcase, beside their bed, on their mantle or on their coffee table, where they often lie unread.

Even those who do read the Bible leave the vast majority of it unread. If you took only the pages that a person actually read in a particular year and made a new Bible out of it, it would be a very thin Bible!

Even many pastors and teachers ignore much of the Bible, partly because there are things found therein which do not fit their personal philosophy or theology or are not what they think should be in the Bible. Consequently, they leave large portions neglected and unread.

For example, many things described in the Old Testament indicate that God is a God of war and a God of anger. This image is not in keeping with the picture of God in the New Testament, where He appears to be more of a merciful God. However, the Bible says that God is the same yesterday, today and forever (Hebrews 13:8).

Since He does not change, this means that He must be *both* the warlike God of the Old Testament and the loving God of the New Testament. In the same way, our earthly fathers at times are loving with us and at times they exhibit the heavy hand of discipline when we need it. So it is with our heavenly Father: at times, He is a God of anger and wrath and, at times, a God of mercy, kindness and compassion.

Let me hasten to add that there are many examples of God's lovingkindness in the Old Testament, and the New Testament is not without its portrait of God's wrath. In anger, he killed Ananias and Sapphira for lying about how much they got for the property they had sold (Acts 5:1-11). We see even more of the vengeance of God unleashed in the book of Revelation. So we begin to see that all of the characteristics of God are found in both the Old and the New Testaments. However, in the Old Testament, we see a great deal more revealed on certain aspects of God's character than we find in the New Testament.

THE OLD TESTAMENT
AND THE NEW TESTAMENT

With Jesus Christ came a new way to become rightly related to God. What we need to realize, however, is that even though the method of rightly relating to God changed, God did not change. His character is still the same today as it was in the Old Testament.

The things that God disliked in the Old Testament, He still dislikes. If adultery displeased Him then, the same is true today. If disobeying His commands made Him angry in the Old Testament, it still does today. If He took vengence on people in the Old Testament, it is unrealistic to presume that He will always react with mercy in every situation today.   His character does not change.

We are obviously not under the Old Testament law—which required the sacrificing of pigeons, lambs and bulls—but God still wants us to give him the first fruits of our labor. Sacrifices are no longer required because Jesus Christ was the once-and-for-all sacrifice for our sins. However, God still wants us to honor Him and to look to Jesus to have our sins forgiven.

Many of the examples in this book are taken from the Old Testament, but they are just as relevant to us today as they were then. They are not relevant in a legalistic sense, but because they help to reveal to us God's heart and character. The Bible tells us several places that God does not change. For example:

6 "For I, the Lord, do not change; therefore you, O sons of Jacob, are not consumed. . . ."
—Malachi 3

17 Every good thing betowed and every perfect gift is from above, coming down from the Father of lights, with whom there is no variation, or shifting shadow.
—James 1

Even though God does not change, we often try to change God. For example, if we do not believe in smoking, we add to the character of God the characteristic that He is against smoking, even though the Bible is silent on that specific subject. If we do not believe in drinking wine, then we add the characteristic to God that He is against drinking wine, even though that belief is contrary to what we find in the Scriptures. If we are against masturbation, we make this part of our image of God as well, even though the Bible is totally silent on the subject. If we like to gossip and spread stories, then we believe that the God that we are remolding in our image approves of our gossiping under the rationalization of "warning the flock."

Do you see what has happened? The God that we have modified in our minds and are worshiping has all of these added characteristics and, thus, is not the real God of the Bible. Most Christians take only the New Testament descriptions of God and His love, mercy and grace, and they totally reject the characteristics of His wrath, anger and punishment depicted in the Old Testament. However, God still has *both*, because He does not change.

Hopefully, this book will help you find the real God of the Bible, and by doing this, to put aside the modified image of God that you may have created in your own mind, who has only the characteristics that you would like for Him to have. Together let's find out what His real characteristics are, according to the Bible.

AS WE EXAMINE THE BIBLE

In this book, we would like to examine some of the things that are in the Bible that many people either have never read or have read and would prefer simply to ignore. This is not intended to be a balanced book, giving both sides of the characteristics of God or of particular situations. There have been innumerable books written giving just the "good" side. This book will concentrate on the little-known facts, and then will leave it up to the reader to balance that with all the other things that he has heard and read.

There is probably something in this book that will offend every reader. However, remember that I am not writing about things from my imagination. Rather, I am simply quoting from the Bible and relating events and ideas from it. My hope and my prayer is that, by reading this book, you will become more balanced in your view of God and in your view of what is contained in the Bible, rather than having a sugar-coated picture of this very down-to-earth book and what it teaches.

Before we conclude this opening chapter, I feel compelled to add an additional thought about the Old Testament. Many teachers—particularly those who adhere to the dispensational theory—tend to minimize the Old Testament. In reality, they regard it as not being very relevant to us. However, even though we are not under the Old Testament Law, I think the Old Testament is indeed for us. Paul makes this very clear in writing to the churches at Corinth and Rome:

> 4 For whatever was written in earlier times was written for our instruction, that through perseverance and the encouragement of the Scriptures we might have hope.
> —Romans 15

> 11 Now these things happened to them as an example, and they were written for our instruction, upon whom the ends of the ages have come.
> —1 Corinthians 10

The Old Testament was written for our instruction, and we should not ignore it.

When Jesus Christ was here on the earth, the "Scriptures" were just the Old Testament. He had this to say in response to a question posed to him:

> 29 But Jesus answered and said to them, "You are mistaken, not understanding the Scriptures, or the power of God. . . ."
> —Matthew 22

This was toward the end of His ministry and He was telling the Sadducees that they absolutely needed to understand the Old Testament as well as the power of God. So, I trust that you will want to follow Jesus' counsel here and try to understand the Old Testament Scriptures, the ones that He Himself used and understood. They give us a vital understanding of some of the characteristics of God that we do not find in the New Testament. (For my dispensational friends, please note that this was after Matthew 12).

Now, let us proceed to take a look at this other side of God.

2

THE OTHER SIDE OF GOD

As we go through life, we have the opportunity to meet a number of people. Of those people that we meet, some we choose to get to know and others we do not. A great deal of our life is determined by the choices we make regarding whom we get to know.

Before we talk about getting to know God, I would like to share with you about an individual I was reading about the other day. He had some characteristics that most people would consider highly undesirable. He had given some people poisoned water to drink and it killed a number of them. He had a couple of guys working for him and he forced one of them to kill a bunch of his neighbors. He forced another one to murder a high government official. (This is not very well known.)

He was evidently involved with evil spirits and had the power to order them about. There is evidence that he sent an evil spirit to a particular guy and caused him to go crazy.

Some people say that the reason he did all these "terrible things" was because he was vengeful. If someone did something against him that offended him, he would punish that person severely in return.

Would you like to get to know such a person? What would you say if your children wanted to

become friends with an individual like him? Would
you discourage them from getting to know him?
What would you say to them?

You might pause here for a moment and think
through what your answers to these questions would
be. Many Christians would say that we should get
to know God and certainly not an individual such as
the one described above. Yet what many Christians
do not realize is that the individual just described,
who did all these things, *was God*, as we will see in
just a moment.

God *is* loving and merciful; these are characteristics of God that we like to emphasize. Yet if
that is all we believe about Him, we have a very
slanted 'and unrealistic picture of God. Most
people read about God mainly in the New Testament
and ignore the picture of Him that is found in the
Old Testament. Yet all of the characteristics of
God from the Old Testament are still true of Him,
because God never changes (Malachi 3:6). I would
like to help you develop a more rounded and
complete picture of our God and Father.

Let's first look at some passages in the Bible
that describe some of the things that God did in
Old Testament times. The first passage we will
discuss is found in Jeremiah:

> 13   And the LORD said, "Because they have
> forsaken My law which I set before them and
> have not obeyed My voice nor walked accord-
> ing to it,
> 14   but have walked after the stubbornness
> of their heart and after the Baals, as their
> fathers taught them,"
> 15   therefore thus says the LORD of hosts,
> the God of Israel, "behold, I will feed them,
> this people, with wormwood and give them
> poisoned water to drink. . . ."
> —Jeremiah 9

We see in this passage that the Lord God gave some people poisoned water to drink.

After the children of Israel had come out of Egypt, as we all know, they had Aaron make them a golden calf.   When Moses came down off the mountain and saw this, here is what transpired:

> 25   Now when Moses saw that the people were out of control—for Aaron had let them get out of control to be a derision among their enemies—
>
> 26   then Moses stood in the gate of the camp, and said, "Whoever is for the LORD, come to me!"   And all the sons of Levi gathered together to him.
>
> 27   And he said to them, "Thus says the LORD, the God of Israel, 'Every man of you put his sword upon his thigh and go back and forth from gate to gate in the camp, and kill every man his brother, and every man his friend, and every man his neighbor.'"
>
> 28   So the sons of Levi did as Moses instructed, and about three thousand men of the people fell that day.
>
> 29   Then Moses said, "Dedicate yourselves today to the LORD—for every man has been against his son and against his brother—in order that He may bestow a blessing upon you today."
>
> —Exodus 32

God, through Moses, commanded that the sons of Levi kill everyone who was worshiping the golden calf, whether it be his neighbor or even his brother.   Verse 29 says that everyone who did that would receive a blessing from God.   We will see more about why God did this later.

The bloody scene of the sons of Levi taking their swords and either running them through the stomach of one of the idol worshipers or cutting

off someone's head, even if it were someone that
the sword bearer loved, is hard for us even to
stomach as a scene, much less to acknowledge it as
being something that God Himself ordered. Yet this
is the same God whom we know and love and
serve. He has not changed.

Most Christians have heard and read about
demons and evil spirits. After King Saul had sinned
and Samuel had anointed David as the replacement
king for Saul, God took his revenge on Saul. We
normally think of evil spirits as being directed and
controlled by Satan, so what we find in 1 Samuel 16
may be surprising to many people:

> **14   Now the Spirit of the LORD departed
> from Saul, and an evil spirit from the LORD
> terrorized him.**
> **15   Saul's   servants   then   said   to   him,
> "Behold   now,   an   evil   spirit   from   God   is
> terrorizing you.**
> **16   "Let   our   lord   now   command   your
> servants who are before you. Let them seek a
> man who is a skillful player on the harp; and
> it shall come about when the evil spirit from
> God is on you, that he shall play the harp
> with his hand, and you will be well."**
> **—1 Samuel 16**

Here we see that God Himself sent an evil
spirit to torment and terrorize Saul. In fact, the
spirit drove him to do crazy things, as we read in
1 Samuel 18:

> **10   Now it came about on the next day
> that an evil spirit from God came mightily
> upon Saul, and he raved in the midst of the
> house, while David was playing the harp with
> his hand, as usual; and a spear was in Saul's
> hand.**
> **11   And   Saul   hurled   the   spear   for   he**

thought, "I will pin David to the wall." But
David escaped from his presence twice.

GOD TAKES VENGEANCE

In these particular situations that we have just
examined, the people disobeyed or displeased God
and He took vengeance on them and punished them
severely.   In some cases, the punishment actually
invovled their physical death.

Many of us have often read this familiar verse
in Romans 12:

> 19   Never take your own revenge, beloved,
> but leave room for the wrath of God, for it is
> written, "VENGEANCE IS MINE, I WILL
> REPAY," says the LORD.

However, when we see the wrath of God and
the vengeance of God described in graphic detail in
the Old Testament, we have a hard time handling it.

THE FEAR OF THE LORD IS
THE BEGINNING OF WISDOM

Would you like to be wise? Of course you
would, and so would I.   The Bible says that the
place to begin in acquiring wisdom is to "fear the
Lord."   People have   tried to whitewash or soften
the word "fear" and to change it to words like
"respect." I believe that if the writers of the Bible
had meant "respect," they would have said "respect."
I think "fear" means plain-old-vanilla *fear*. Children
"fear" their parents because they know there is a
spanking that comes if they do not obey them.   If
we want wisdom, we should have that same sort of
fear of God, knowing that He has in the past and
still does punish disobedience.

In no way is this an attempt to take away
from the loving, forgiving, merciful side of God.

What we are trying to do is to bring out the neglected side of God's character that we do not particularly like to look at. God has many facets. He is tender, loving, and forgiving, and yet He is also a God of wrath, punishment, revenge and violence against those who disobey Him. Many times the Scriptures tell us that He is a jealous God (Exodus 34:14, for example).

Looking further at this neglected side of God's nature, among other things, we find that God:

1. Ordered a man (Abraham) to kill his favorite son (Genesis 22:1,2).

2. Said that He would visit His wrath unto the fourth generation, so that even unborn babies would be punished for their grandfather's sins (Deuteronomy 5:9).

3. Killed the oldest child of all the Egyptians, whether or not they were against the Israelites leaving their country (Exodus 13:15).

4. Sent a flood that killed everyone, except a small handful of people and animals. This means that little babies just a day or two old and the elderly were all drowned in the flood (Genesis 7:5-22).

5. Destroyed Sodom and Gomorrah by fire. Here again, even newborn babies were killed, along with everyone else (Genesis 19:24,25).

SPOILED CHILDREN

If parents are only gentle and forgiving and never punish and spank their children, the children wind up spoiled rotten and they are a pain to be around. "Spare the rod and spoil the child," as the saying goes. According to Proverbs 13:24, a parent who "spares the rod" hates his children, while those who really love their children discipline them diligently.

If God the Father were all sweetness and tenderness, and the fear of the paddle were removed, Christians would become like spoiled children. Unfortunately, I think that is probably a description of some of the people in the Christian church in America today. They are spiritually soft and flabby; all they feel they have to do is "positively confess" and they can get what they want.

What these individuals do not realize is that the disciplining hand of God is being raised, and it is about to fall. Unfortunately, when they do get a rare spanking, many spoiled children tell their human father, "You don't love me anymore." (Do we do the same with God?)

Obviously it is not true, but the child feels this very strongly. When I was a small boy, I remember my mother spanking me and telling me that it hurt her worse than it did me. I used to think that was a bunch of baloney, but now I understand what she meant.

Whether the Father is dealing with us gently or spanking us, in either case, He is showing us how much He loves us. In either role, He is holy, righteous and abhors that which is evil. He would never lead anyone to do anything that is evil, *according to HIS standards*. But His ways are not our ways, and His thoughts are not our thoughts (Isaiah 55:8, 9). Thus, some of the things that He may tell us to do can be confusing to us, as they possibly were to Abraham, Joshua, Elijah, Ehud and others whom God asked to be instruments of His vengeance or to do things that were illogical according to human reasoning.

In no way does looking at this more realistic view of God give license to sin, to do wrong or evil. What we are seeking to do is to get to know God as He really is.

GET TO KNOW THE REAL GOD

I would encourage you to read through the
following books of the Old Testament and to ask
God to show you afresh what He is really like:

Genesis	1 & 2 Kings
Exodus	Job
Joshua	Psalms
Judges	Jeremiah
1 & 2 Samuel	Ezekiel

We tend to emphasize the loving, forgiving,
merciful God and ignore all of the other aspects of
His character. We emphasize the characteristics of
God that we think are "good" and skip over those
that we would consider "less good" or, if we were
really honest with ourselves, we would almost
consider them "evil."

Remember, God *is* a loving, kind and forgiving
God. However, He also has another side, and we
have simply touched briefly on that side of God's
character, with which some people either are not
familiar or do not care to acknowledge. We will
get into some of these aspects of the character of
God in more detail in later chapters.

It is enough to say here that God loves you
and wants you to have eternal life. He was willing
to send His Son, Jesus Christ, to take your
punishment for you. However, He is still a God of
judgment and wrath and will punish evil deeds.

Speaking of evil deeds, before we proceed,
one subject we need to discuss is the first sin in
the world, which was acquiring the "knowledge of
good and evil."

3

KNOWLEDGE
OF GOOD AND EVIL

We now need to discuss a bedrock foundational truth that I have rarely seen taught, either in books or from a pulpit.

It deals with the first commandment given to men; therefore, God must have thought it was very important. It was the prohibition against gaining knowledge of good and evil. It has far more implications than one might realize, so stay with me as we go back and review the two special trees in the garden of Eden.

4 This is the account of the heavens and the earth when they were created, in the day that the LORD God made earth and heaven.

5 Now no shrub of the field was yet in the earth, and no plant of the field had yet sprouted, for the LORD God had not sent rain upon the earth; and there was no man to cultivate the ground.

6 But a mist used to rise from the earth and water the whole surface of the ground.

7 Then the LORD God formed man of dust from the ground, and breathed into his nostrils the breath of life; and man became a living being.

>   8   And the LORD God planted a garden
> toward the east, in Eden; and there He placed
> the man whom He had formed.
>   9   And out of the ground the LORD God
> caused to grow every tree that is pleasing to
> the sight and good for food, the tree of life
> also in the midst of the garden, and the tree
> of the knowledge of good and evil.
>   —Genesis 2

As we can see in this passage, there were
many trees of all kinds in the garden of Eden. But
there were two special trees:

1.   The tree of life
2.   The tree of the knowledge of good and
     evil

As we all know, God forbade Adam and Eve to
eat of the tree of the knowledge of good and evil,
as is recorded further in Genesis 2:

>   15   Then the LORD God took the man and
> put him into the garden of Eden to cultivate it
> and keep it.
>   16   And the LORD God commanded the
> man, saying, "From any tree of the garden you
> may eat freely;
>   17   but from the tree of the knowledge of
> good and evil you shall not eat, for in the day
> that you eat from it you shall surely die."

In Genesis 3, we find God casting Adam and
Eve out of the garden so that they could not eat of
the tree of life.

>   22   Then the LORD God said, "Behold, the
> man has become like one of Us, knowing good
> and evil; and now lest he stretch out his hand,

and take also from the tree of life, and eat,
and live forever"—

23   therefore the LORD God sent him out
from the garden of Eden, to cultivate the
ground from which he was taken.

24   So He drove the man out; and at the
east of the garden of Eden he stationed the
cherubim, and the flaming sword which turned
every direction, to guard the way to the tree
of life.

—Genesis 3

The reason God did not want them to eat of
the tree of life is because they had gained
something God never wanted them to have—the
knowledge of good and evil.

The fall of Adam and Eve involves much more
than the sin of disobeying God. Because of that
sin, they gained the knowledge of good and evil. If
gaining the knowledge of good and evil is such a
terrible thing that God cast them out of the garden,
we need to understand why it is so bad and find
out if it is also bad for you and me.

YOU CAN KNOW GOD OR GOOD AND EVIL
BUT NOT BOTH

I have first stated the conclusion—"you can
know God *or* good and evil, but not both"—and
would now like to present the evidence for it. This
is a fairly bold statement that requires close
examination.

Before they ate of the forbidden fruit of the
tree of the knowledge of good and evil, Adam and
Eve could make decisions such as naming the
animals, but for any moral decision, they had to ask
God. Evidently He walked frequently in the garden
of Eden, and any questions they had concerning
what was right or wrong, good or bad, they simply
asked God and He told them.

He did not want them making their own moral judgments as to what was good and evil based on their own knowledge. This is the reason that He prohibited them from eating of that particular tree. In the worst way, Satan wanted to break this relationship of dependence upon God, as we see recorded in Chapter 3 of Genesis:

1   Now the serpent was more crafty than any beast of the field which the LORD God made. And he said to the woman, "Indeed, has God said, 'You shall not eat from any tree of the garden'?"

2   And the woman said to the serpent, "From the fruit of the trees of the garden we may eat;

3   but from the fruit of the tree which is in the middle of the garden, God has said, "You shall not eat from it or touch it, lest you die."'

4   And the serpent said to the woman, "You surely shall not die!

5   For God knows that in the day you eat from it your eyes will be opened, and you will be like God, knowing good and evil."

6   When the woman saw that the tree was good for food, and that it was a delight to the eyes, and that the tree was desirable to make one wise, she took from its fruit and ate; and she gave also to her husband with her, and he ate.

7   Then the eyes of both of them were opened, and they knew that they were naked; and they sewed fig leaves together and made themselves loin coverings.

8   And they heard the sound of the LORD God walking in the garden in the cool of the day, and the man and his wife hid themselves from the presence of the LORD God among the trees of the garden.

9   Then the LORD God called to the man,
and said to him, "Where are you?"
10   And he said, "I heard the sound of
Thee in the garden, and I was afraid because I
was naked; so I hid myself."
11   And He said, "Who told you that you
were naked?   Have you eaten from the tree of
which I commanded you not to eat?"

—Genesis 3

Adam and Eve had been naked from the
beginning, and evidently neither they nor God had
seen anything wrong with it.   However, once they
ate of the tree of the knowledge of good and evil,
Adam and Eve realized they were naked and
they—by themselves—concluded that it was wrong.
Then they made themselves aprons of leaves to
cover their nakedness.

When God came into the garden, He called
them out from their hiding place.   I can just
imagine Him asking them where they got those silly
clothes, and Adam and Eve responding that they
had made them. God might have asked, "Why did
you make them?   Why did you hide yourselves?"
Adam would have replied, "Because I was naked." I
imagine that God might have responded, "So what?"
Then Adam must have said, "But that is wrong."

God must have wept inside as He asked them
who told them they were naked and what made
them think it was wrong.   He already must have
known the answer, but then He asked them if they
had eaten of the tree of the knowledge of good and
evil.

Before Adam and Eve ate the fruit of the tree
of the knowledge of good and evil, when they had
to make a moral decision they went to God, and
they did whatever He said.   After they ate of it,
they could use their own knowledge, reasoning and
feelings about what was right and wrong to make
these decisions, independent of God.   Either Adam

and Eve could make their decisions based on knowing God and what He told them to do in each specific situation, or they could make decisions based on their knowledge of good and evil, but they couldn't do both. They had chosen to rely on their own knowledge and therefore were cast out of the garden, away from the presence of God and basically away from the guidance of God. Actually, it was because of His mercy that God cast them out of the garden, away from the tree of life, because He did not want them to live forever in their sinful state, relying on their own knowledge instead of on Him.

You could state the principle in this way:

Knowing God and knowing good and evil are mutually exclusive.

We will see the scriptural basis for this when we examine Proverbs 3:5,6. Another example of this principle is the Pharisees. Certainly the Pharisees knew what was right and wrong and what was good and evil, but they did not know God.

13 "But woe to you, scribes and Pharisees, hypocrites, because you shut off the kingdom of heaven from men; for you do not enter in yourselves, nor do you allow those who are entering to go in.
14 "Woe to you, scribes and Pharisees, hypocrites, because you devour widows' houses, even while for a pretense you make long prayers; therefore you shall receive greater condemnation.
15 "Woe to you, scribes and Pharisees, hypocrites, because you travel about on sea and land to make one proselyte, and when he becomes one, you make him twice as much a son of hell as yourselves. . . .

23   "Woe to you, scribes and Pharisees, hypocrites!   For you tithe mint and dill and cummin, and have neglected the weightier provisions of the law; justice and mercy and faithfulness; but these are the things you should have done without neglecting the other.

25   "Woe to you, scribes and Pharisees, hypocrites!   For you clean the outside of the cup and of the dish, but inside they are full of robbery and self-indulgence.

26   "You blind Pharisee, first clean the inside of the cup and of the dish, so that the outside of it may become clean also.

27   "Woe to you, scribes and Pharisees, hypocrites!   For you are like whitewashed tombs which on the outside appear beautiful, but inside they are full of dead men's bones and all uncleanness. . . .

37   "O Jerusalem, Jerusalem, who kills the prophets and stones those who are sent to her! How often I wanted to gather your children together, the way a hen gathers her chicks under her wings, and you were unwilling. . . ."

—Matthew 23

As we can see, Christ condemned the Pharisees who did everything according to their knowledge of good and evil. They were not close to God, did not hear God, and even rejected God's very own Son.

In verse 37 in the passage above from Matthew 23, Christ cries out to the inhabitants of Jerusalem, yearning to gather them in a loving way as a hen gathers her chicks, yearning to reestablish this personal relationship.   But they were so enslaved to their knowledge of good and evil that they could not have a personal relationship with God through His Son, Jesus Christ.

A strong teaching on this subject is found in Proverbs:

> **5** Trust in the Lord with all thine heart; and lean not unto thine own understanding.
> **6** In all thy ways acknowledge him, and he shall direct thy paths.
>
> —Proverbs 3, KJV

These verses admonish us to do three things:

1. Trust in the Lord with all our heart
2. Lean not to our own understanding
3. In all our ways acknowledge Him

If we do those three things, then God promises that He will guide us. He shall direct our paths. The second of these three requirements is by far the hardest. It is that we do not lean to our understanding, and I believe this means our understanding of what is good and evil, or right and wrong. The smarter an individual is, the more difficult this is for him. But the strong implication is that you can either have God guide your paths *or* you can lean to your own understanding, but you cannot do both.

Many churches teach things like: "Do not handle this," "Do not taste that," "Do not touch the other." This kind of instruction is based on their knowledge of good and evil, which they try to impose upon their members. These people mean well, but they forget what Colossians 2 says on this:

> **20** If you have died with Christ to the elementary principles of the world, why, as if you were living in the world, do you submit yourself to decrees, such as
> **21** "Do not handle, do not taste, do not touch!"
> **22** (which all refer to things destined to perish with the using)—in accordance with the commandments and teachings of men?

23 These are matters which have, to be
sure, the appearance of wisdom in self-made
religion and self-abasement and severe treat-
ment of the body, but are of no value against
fleshly indulgence.

—Colossians 2

As we can see from these verses, having these
lists of "do's" and "don'ts" gives an appearance of
widsom, but the Bible says they are of *no value*
against fleshly indulgence.   In other words, the
knowledge of good and evil will never keep us from
sinning and indulging in things of the flesh.
Knowing God and having a close personal relationship with Him will keep us from indulging in these
fleshly things.   So once again, we see that knowing
God and knowing good and evil are mutually
exclusive.

KNOWLEDGE OF GOOD AND EVIL
CAN PREVENT US FROM OBEYING GOD

It is interesting to note that our knowledge of
good and evil can cause us to sin (sin being
disobedience to God).   This sounds like an incredible statement, but put yourself in the place of
Abraham.   What if God told you to go out and kill
or sacrifice your only or your favorite child?
Most of us would argue with God and say, "But
God, that is wrong."   Our knowledge of good and
evil would prevent us from obeying God.

It is not only our knowledge of good and evil
that can keep us from obeying God; it is also our
logical mind (which perhaps is just another facet of
the knowledge of good and evil).   For example,
Abraham was living in the Ur of the Chaldees in
what was a luxurious home for his time.   (This
home, which has been excavated, was a two-story
brick home, which one can visit today if one can
get into Iraq.)   He had a very comfortable life and

was evidently very content when God told him to pack up everything and to "Go West, young man," to a land that He would show him. Abraham did not even know where he was going, nor how he would get there, nor how he would recognize it when he arrived!

To many of Abraham's friends, I am sure this was a stupid, illogical and insane thing to do. God frequently asks us to do things that don't seem logical or that seem to violate our sense of what is right and wrong. Many people, had they been in Abraham's situation, would have allowed their knowledge of good and evil to prevent them from leaving their plush homes, businesses and surroundings to become nomads living in tents. You might even ask yourself the question, if God asked you right now to leave everything you own and, taking a minimum of possessions, to start moving north or south, living in a tent, what would you do?

Baptism is an interesting example of what we are discussing. If someone stands up in front of a church and publicly declares that he has received Jesus Christ as his Savior, there is absolutely no logical reason to be baptized. I believe that at the very beginning of our Christian life Jesus asks us to do something that is illogical and to do it simply because He asks us to. This is to prepare us so that when He later asks us to do very difficult things that are illogical, we will be used to obeying.

God has asked me to do a number of highly illogical things. As I was moving up the IBM management ladder, He said; "Take a year's leave of absence and go live on Catalina Island in a cove, where there is no electricity or telephones, and no roads into the place, and be a caretaker at a camp." I did this, and God tremendously blessed it. Later, I was living in Los Angeles and God told me to move to Canada. There was no logical reason to move to Canada but I did so, and there I found my wife, Jeani. I am absolutely convinced that He took me to Canada just to find her. Many Christians would have allowed their logical reasoning of good and evil to prevent them from obeying God in these and many similar situations.

You might say: "But Abraham lived before the Ten Commandments. God asked him to sacrifice his son before the commandment 'thou shalt not kill' was given." All right, let's take a look at what happened *after* the Ten Commandments were given in Exodus 20. We find this recorded in Joshua 10, for example:

> 40 Thus Joshua struck all of the land, the hill country and the Negev and the lowland and the slopes and all their kings. He left no survivor, but he utterly destroyed all who breathed, just as the Lord, the God of Israel, had commanded.
>
> —Joshua 10

Had you been there and had you been part of Joshua's army, would you have strapped on your sword and gone out, under God's command, to kill all those people (including old or pregnant women and little babies)?

We also read in Chapter 2 how Moses and the sons of Levi killed everyone who was worshiping the golden calf, after Moses came down from the mountain and found the people in rebellion against God. Would you have obeyed God, as the sons of Levi did, to kill those who were sinning by worshiping that idol? Many Christians living in the United States today would have refused to obey God, because their "knowledge of good and evil" would have told them that it was wrong.

LESSONS FROM ELIJAH

We might excuse Moses and the sons of Levi from these types of acts—and perhaps even Joshua.

However, our knowledge of good and evil would
have caused most of us to refuse to be a part of it.
The same would be true of the victorious time at
Jericho, when God caused the walls to fall down.
Every one of God's children there went forward
into the city over the crumbled walls and, at God's
command, killed all of those in the city; Rahab the
harlot and those who were with her in her house
were the only ones left alive. You might discount
this because Joshua was the military leader of his
people.   That's true, but he was under marching
orders from God.

So let's go to a man that we would all
consider a true prophet and a man of God, Elijah.
No doubt we have all studied and rejoiced in the
fact that Elijah had the contest with 450 of Baal's
prophets, and that God honored him by bringing fire
down from heaven and consuming the sacrifice, the
wood, and even the water in the trench.   All
rejoiced in God's power and victory.   But we tend
to stop before the end of the story:

> 22 Then Elijah said to the people, "I alone
> am left a prophet of the LORD, but Baal's
> prophets are 450 men. . . ."

> 36 Then it came about at the time of the
> offering of the evening sacrifice, that Elijah
> the prophet came near and said, "O, LORD,
> the God of Abraham, Isaac and Israel, today
> let it be known that Thou art God in Israel,
> and that I am Thy servant, and that I have
> done all these things at Thy word.
> 37 "Answer me, O LORD, answer me, that
> this people may know that Thou,   O LORD, art
> God, and that Thou hast turned their heart
> back again."
> 38 Then the fire of the Lord fell, and
> consumed the burnt offering and the wood and
> the stones and the dust, and licked up the
> water that was in the trench. . . .

40 Then Elijah said to them, "Seize the
prophets of Baal; do not let one of them
escape." So they seized them; and Elijah
brought them down to the brook Kishon, and
slew them there.

—1 Kings 18

At the end of the story, Elijah had to kill the
false prophets of Baal. It is all part of the story.
God did not want false religions or priests of false
religions around to pollute His people. Many of us
would love to have been there and prayed and seen
the fire come down from heaven, but likely, because
of our knowledge of good and evil, we would have
refused to have killed the 450 false prophets of
Baal. Perhaps that is why we do not have the
power of God like Elijah did, because we want to
obey God selectively, based on our own knowledge
of good and evil.

God also gave Elijah the power to bring down
literal fire from heaven and consume enemies, and
God expected him to use this power as He directed.
This was not any theoretical or mystical fire. This
was actual fire that burned and killed:

9 Then the king sent to him a captain of
fifty with his fifty. And he went up to him,
and behold, he was sitting on the top of the
hill. And he said to him, "O man of God, the
king says, 'Come down.'"
10 And Elijah answered and said to the
captain of fifty, "If I am a man of God, let
fire come down from heaven and consume you
and your fifty." Then fire came down from
heaven and consumed him and his fifty.
11 So he again sent to him another captain
of fifty with his fifty. And he answered and
said to him, "O man of God, thus says the
king, 'Come down quickly.'"

12 And Elijah answered and said to them, "If I am a man of God, let fire come down from heaven and consume you and your fifty." Then the fire of God came down from heaven and consumed him and his fifty.

13 So he again sent the captain of a third fifty with his fifty. When the third captain of fifty went up, he came and bowed down on his knees before Elijah, and begged him and said to him, "O man of God, please let my life and the lives of these fifty servants of yours be precious in your sight.

14 "Behold fire came down from heaven, and consumed the first two captains of fifty with their fifties; but now let my life be precious in your sight."

15 And the angel of the Lord said to Elijah, "Go down with him; do not be afraid of him." So he arose and went down with him to the king.

—2 Kings 1

You may think: "Well, this was all in the Old Testament. Nothing like this would ever occur in the New Testament." I would like to take two examples from the New Testament. The first one fits right in with what we have been discussing about Elijah. It is found in Revelation 11:

3 "And I will grant authority to my two witnesses, and they will prophesy for twelve hundred and sixty days, clothed in sackcloth."

4 These are the two olive trees and the two lampstands that stand before the Lord of the earth.

5 And if anyone desires to harm them, fire proceeds out of their mouth and devours their enemies; and if anyone would desire to harm them, in this manner he must be killed.

6 These have the power to shut up the
sky; in order that rain may not fall during the
days of their prophesying; and they have
power over the waters to turn them into
blood, and to smite the earth with every
plague, as often as they desire.

Here we see that God is again going to give
the kind of "fire power" that Elijah had; the two
witnesses (and I believe this most likely refers to
two groups of people, not two individuals) will have
power to call down fire from heaven to destroy
their enemies. Unfortunately, most Christians could
miss becoming part of these two witness companies,
because their knowledge of good and evil would
prevent them from calling down fire from heaven to
destroy their enemies, if God were to ask them to
do such a thing.

Let me hasten to reaffirm that in no way am I
for killing. I hate it. I would hate to be forced to
do it. What I am saying is that I want to be
willing to obey my God whatever He tells me to do
in the turbulent times ahead.

I have taken many of these examples involving
killing as an extreme illustration of the principle to
help you realize the significance of what we are
talking about. Now let's turn to an example that
might be more likely for many people to experience:

1 "Then the kingdom of heaven will be
comparable to ten virgins, who took their
lamps, and went out to meet the bridegroom.
2 "And five of them were foolish, and
five were prudent.
3 "For when the foolish took their lamps,
they took no oil with them,
4 but the prudent took oil in flasks along
with their lamps.
5 "Now while the bridegroom was delay-
ing, they all got drowsy and began to sleep.

6 "But at midnight there was a shout, 'Behold the bridegroom! Come out to meet him.'

7 "Then all those virgins rose, and trimmed their lamps.

8 "And the foolish said to the prudent, 'Give us some of your oil, for our lamps are going out.'

9 "But the prudent answered, saying, 'No, there will not be enough for us and you too; go instead to the dealers and buy some for yourselves.'

10 "And while they were going away to make the purchase, the bridegroom came, and those who were ready went in with him to the wedding feast; and the door was shut.

11 "And later the other virgins also came, saying, Lord, Lord, open up for us.'

12 "But He answered and said, 'Truly I say to you, I do not know you.'

13 "Be on the alert then, for you do not know the day nor the hour. . . ."

—Matthew 25

If most Christians today were one of the five virgins who had surplus oil, and the other five virgins who had run out of oil came to them, they would think that the "Christian thing to do" would be to share their surplus oil with them. This concept is based on the knowledge of good and evil. However, as Christ teaches, in this instance it would have been sin for the five wise virgins, who had prepared ahead and brought extra oil, to have shared their oil with the foolish ones, who had made no preparation.

Here once more, we can see that our knowledge of good and evil could have caused us to sin. It is difficult to think of sharing as a sin, but anything we do can be sin if it is not what God is telling us to do.

For the times of crisis ahead, God may have led you to prepare by storing extra food, water or something else. If He tells you to share, praise God! Give some or all of it away, as He directs. If He tells you not to share, then don't do it. We must take our orders directly from Him and not make our decisions based on our knowledge of good and evil, our logic.

We could take many other examples from both the Old and New Testaments. It would have been sin for Noah to let additional people into the ark, for example, even though they were dying and pounding on the door. On the other hand, it would have been sin for the widow lady (and her son) not to share the flour and oil with God's prophet (1 Kings 17:11-16).

We like to make little rules for ourselves, such as "it is always good to share" or "it is never good to drink wine." Do you see what we are doing? Once we say that we will *always* do this or we will *never* do that, God can no longer lead us in that area of our lives. Our well-meaning rules take precedence over God's leading.

In the Bible, there are times when it glorified God to share and times when it would have been sin. There are times when God has asked one of His servants to call down fire to destroy enemies and other times when it would have been sin to do that. We can not depend on our rules or our knowledge of good and evil. We must listen to God's voice on each occasion and do what He tells us to do.

YOUR KNOWLEDGE OF GOOD AND EVIL
CAN PREVENT YOU FROM BENEFITTING
FROM THIS BOOK

The things contained in the subsequent chapters of this book may astound you or surprise you. Many of the things that we will be discussing may cause you to think, "That shouldn't be in the Bible." Or you might think, "God wouldn't or shouldn't do that."

Please do not let your knowledge of good and evil—what you think is right or wrong, or what you think God should or shouldn't do—blind you to the fact of what God actually *did* and what God actually *said*.

Many things in these next chapters will be very difficult for you to believe, if you do not read it in the Bible for yourself. Therefore, we have actually printed the scriptural passages for your convenience. We would encourage you later on to take your own Bible and reread those same passages in the broader context.

Now, let us proceed to explore some of the strange and amazing things that are found in the Bible. They may be hard to believe but, believe it or not, *"it's in the book."*

4

NEW MOON FESTIVALS

What would you think if you started visiting a church and they had a special worship or praise service everytime there was a new moon? Would it raise any questions in your mind? Many Christians would react negatively. Let us pause and see what the Bible has to say before we react.

The occult, which includes astrology, is forbidden in the Bible. We will have more to say about that in a later chapter. However, most people are unaware that God commanded offerings to be made at the time of the new moons:

> 3 He also appointed the king's portion of his goods for the burnt offerings, namely, for the morning and evening burnt offerings, and the burnt offerings for the sabbaths and for the new moons and for the fixed festivals, as it is written in the law of the Lord.
>
> —2 Chronicles 31

Furthermore, the main times for truly committing the people to God in the Old Testament were on the:

1. Sabbath
2. New moons
3. Three annual feasts

> 12 Then Solomon offered burnt offerings to
> the Lord on the altar of the Lord which he
> had built before the porch;
> 13 and did so according to the daily rule,
> offering them up according to the command-
> ment of Moses, for the sabbaths, the new
> moons, and the three annual feasts—the Feast
> of Unleavened Bread, the Feast of Weeks, and
> the Feast of Booths.
>
> —2 Chronicles 8

God put the times of the new moon right up
there along with the Sabbath and the three major
feasts in the Old Testament.   There is much
written, said and done about celebrating a day of
rest each week and, in some circles, celebrating the
three major feasts in the Old Testament. However,
very little is said or done about celebrating at the
new moon, in spite of the fact that God commanded
it.

This thought was also expressed as Solomon
was preparing to build the temple of God:

> 4 "Behold, I am about to build a house for
> the name of the Lord my God, dedicating it to
> Him, to burn fragrant incense before Him, and
> to set out the showbread continually, and to
> offer burnt offerings morning and evening, on
> sabbaths and on new moons and on the ap-
> pointed feasts of the Lord our God, this
> being required forever in Israel.
> 5 "And the house which I am about to
> build will be great; for greater is our God
> than all the gods. . . ."
>
> —2 Chronicles 2

David himself had given this same instruction
to the people:

25 For David said, "The Lord God of Israel has given rest to His people, and He dwells in Jerusalem forever. . . .

30 And they are to stand every morning to thank and to praise the Lord, and likewise at evening,
31 and to offer all burnt offerings to the Lord, on the sabbaths, the new moons and the fixed festivals in the number set by the ordinance concerning them, continually before the Lord.

—1 Chronicles 23

Evidently this new moon festival was a festival celebrated regularly by King Saul, because it is apparent from the following passage that David would have been missed if he did not show up:

5 So David said to Jonathan, "Behold, tomorrow is the new moon, and I ought to sit down to eat with the king. But let me go, that I may hide myself in the field until the third evening. . . .

18 Then Jonathan said to him, "Tomorrow is the new moon, and you will be missed because your seat will be empty. . . .

24 So David hid in the field; and when the new moon came, the king sat down to eat food.
25 And the king sat on his seat as usual, the seat by the wall; then Jonathan rose up and Abner sat down by Saul's side, but David's place was empty.
26 Nevertheless Saul did not speak anything that day, for he thought, "It is an accident, he is not clean, surely he is not clean."
27 And it came about the next day, the second day of the new moon, that David's place was empty; so Saul said to Jonathan his

son, "Why has the son of Jesse not come to
the meal, either yesterday or today?"

—1 Samuel 20

Not all the Psalms were written by David. In
a Psalm written by Asaph, we find this:

1   Sing for joy to God our strength;
    Shout joyfully to the God of Jacob.
2   Raise a song, strike the timbrel,
    The sweet sounding lyre with the harp.
3   Blow the trumpet at the new moon,
    At the full moon, on our feast day
4   For it is a statute for Israel,
    An ordinance of the God of Jacob.

—Psalm 81

Here the psalmist tells us that we are to sing
for joy to our God, to shout joyfully to Him and to
make music with the timbrel, the lyre and the harp,
However, it also says that we are to blow the
trumpet at the new moon.

God Himself talks about this new moon feast.

9   'Thus says the Lord God, "Enough, you
princes of Israel; put away violence and
destruction, and practice justice and righteousness.   Stop your expropriations from My
people," declares the Lord God. . . .'

17   "And it shall be the prince's part to
provide   the   burnt   offerings,   the   grain
offerings,   and   the   libations   at   the   feasts,   on
the new moons, and on the sabbaths, at all the
appointed   feasts   of   the   house   of   Israel;   he
shall   provide   the   sin   offering,   the   grain
offering,   the   burnt   offering,   and   the   peace
offerings,   to   make   atonement   for   the   house   of
Israel."

—Ezekiel 45

Here God commands the prince of the land not only to have a feast on the new moons, on the Sabbaths and on the three appointed feasts, but the prince is to provide the offerings and the libations. God goes on to say:

> 3 "The people of the land shall also worship at the doorway of that gate before the Lord on the sabbaths and on the new moons. . . ."

—Ezekiel 46

WHY DID GOD WANT
NEW MOON FESTIVALS?

Years ago, when I taught computer concepts to executives, I would tell them at the very beginning of the course that the only questions that I would not answer were questions that began with the words "what if." For example, suppose 32 meant "subtract" in the computer and 34 meant "add." If they asked, "What if I put in 33?", the only way I would be able to answer that question was if I went and tried it myself, and they could try it just as easily. Therefore, I told them I would refuse to answer those kinds of questions.

Similarly, in teaching Bible courses, I have stated that the only questions I would not attempt to answer were questions that started with "Why did God?" The reason I said this is that when we try to figure out why God did certain things, we are putting ourselves in a superior position to God, trying to look down and understand His thoughts and motivations and judge whether or not there was a different or a better way. This is the height of egotism, if an individual thinks that he can answer questions about God's motivation for everything that He does.

For example, many people might ask questions such as these:

Why did God tilt the earth on its axis?
Why does God allow evil?
Why did God not start off with the new
    covenant, if He knew the old covenant
    was not going to work?
Why did God create man first and then
    woman?
Why does God allow people to be born
    deformed?

Of course, this list could go on and on. We all wonder about why God did certain things. The Bible tells us that His ways are above our ways and His thoughts are above our thoughts. What this really says is that there is no way we can comprehend God's mind and realize why He did certain things:

8   "For My thoughts are not your thoughts,
     Neither are your ways My ways,"
         declares the Lord.
9   "For as the heavens are higher than the
     earth,
     So are My ways higher than your ways,
     And My thoughts than your thoughts. . . ."
                                      —Isaiah 55

Most of what we have covered in this book so far has been clearly what the Scriptures have said. I like to differentiate my conjecture from what the Scriptures clearly teach. The following thought is simply conjecture on my part. In praying about why God might want to have a festival at every new moon, the Lord reminded me of the three major feasts of the Old Testament:

The Feast of Passover
The Feast of Pentecost
The Feast of Tabernacles

These feasts were all based on an agricultural society. They were in connection with times of planting and times of harvest. Perhaps one of the reasons God wanted feasts at these particular times was to remind the people when they planted that only He could give the increase, only He could send the rains, and so forth. Then, at the times of harvest, they needed to be reminded that only God was able to give them the abundant harvest and to bless their toils and their labors.

However, the Hebrews in the Old Testament were quite a stubborn and forgetful group. Perhaps the Lord felt that three times a year was not often enough to remind them of their dependence on Him. Thus, after the moon had gone dark and the crescent of a new moon began to show, it could be that God was telling His people once more that He was going to provide for them and that He had everything under control. This was certainly cause for rejoicing.

The Lord may show you something different about why He wanted festivals at the new moon. But now, ever since the Lord showed me this, when I see a new moon, I really have a sense of rejoicing and praise in my heart.

If a church or a group of believers were to celebrate the Lord not only on the day of rest each week, but also at each new moon, many Christians would be shocked and might even accuse them of "moon worship." However, if they did have praise services every time there was a new moon, it would be perfectly in keeping with what was on God's heart and given as one of God's commandments in the Bible. *It's in the book.*

5

ASTROLOGY AND THE OCCULT

Many people, including many Christians, feel that reading the astrology column in the daily newspaper or playing with an Ouija board is harmless fun. However, God considers it a gross wickedness:

10   "And you felt secure in your wicked-
ness and said,
'No one sees me,'
Your wisdom and your knowledge, they
have deluded you;
For you have said in your heart,
'I am, and there is no one besides me.'
11   "But evil will come on you
Which you will not know how to charm
away;
And disaster will fall on you
For which you cannot atone,
And destruction about which you do not
know
Will come on you suddenly.
12   "Stand fast now in your spells
And in your many sorceries
With which you have labored from your
youth;
Perhaps you will be able to profit,
Perhaps you may cause trembling.

13   "You are wearied with your many coun-
         sels;
      Let now the astrologers,
      Those who prophesy by the stars,
      Those who predict by the new moons,
      Stand up and save you from what will
         come upon you.
14   "Behold, they have become like stubble,
      Fire burns them;
      They cannot deliver themselves from
         the power of the flame;
      There will be no coal to warm by,
      Nor a fire to sit before!

                                    —Isaiah 47

The key problem is found in verse 13 above.
There are those who *prophesy* by the stars and
predict by the new moons. It is the prophesying
and predicting based on anything other than God
that is sin. God is a jealous God, and He and He
alone wants to direct your paths.

When we read or receive a prediction about
our lives in some form—about the day, or the near
future or even the distant future—then that
prediction can determine a lot of actions. God
wants His will and His will alone to determine our
actions.

In his Basic Youth Conflict Seminar, Bill
Gothard gives the example of a mother and a
grandmother in a teashop with a seven-year-old
daughter. A lady came by wanting to read the tea
leaves in the cup, and the mother and the
grandmother thought it would be cute to have the
little girl's tea leaves read.

The woman read the tea leaves in the little
girl's cup and predicted that she would marry
someone in uniform, that she would have three
children and they would all be girls. That
seemingly-innocent event affected—no, really *controlled*—the rest of that little girl's life.

She would not date anyone who did not have a uniform, whether it be a band uniform or a postman's uniform, because she knew she was going to marry someone who wore a uniform. She eventually did marry someone who wore a uniform. After they were married, they had two children who were both girls. After that, she had a third child, a son. This girl, who was then a woman, totally rejected that third child, because it was supposed to have been a daughter, according to the tea leaf prediction. Evidently Satan really utilized this, seemingly-innocent event, because that little baby would scream anytime he was near a church, to the extent that they could never take him to church at all.

The supposedly innocent reading of the tea leaves controlled that girl's actions and, according to the Bible, it is a sin to have your actions controlled by something other than God and His will.

It is okay to celebrate the festival of a new moon, according to the Scriptures, but it is a sin to use that new moon for predictive or prophetic value.

Only God speaks the truth. These occult practices may have an element of the truth, but they basically speak lies, and the Bible tells us to not listen to them:

> 9 "But as for you, do not listen to your prophets, your diviners, your dreamers, your soothsayers, or your sorcerers, who speak to you, saying, 'You shall not serve the king of Babylon.'
> 10 "For they prophesy a lie to you, in order to remove you far from your land; and I will drive you out, and you will perish. . . ."
> —Jeremiah 27

DETESTABLE TO GOD

Would you like to be detestable to God? Certainly not. As the children of Israel were about to enter the promised land, God told them that if they did certain things, they would indeed be detestable to Him:

9 "When you enter the land which the Lord your God gives you, you shall not learn to imitate the detestable things of those nations.
10 "There shall not be found among you anyone who makes his son or his daughter pass through the fire, one who uses divination, one who practices witchcraft, or one who interprets omens, or a sorcerer,
11 or one who casts a spell, or a medium, or a spiritist, or one who calls up the dead.
12 "For whoever does these things is detestable to the Lord; and because of these detestable things the Lord your God will drive them out before you.
13 "You shall be blameless before the Lord your God.
14 "For those nations, which you shall dispossess, listen to those who practice witchcraft and to diviners, but as for you, the Lord your God has not allowed you to do so. . . ."
—Deuteronomy 18

As we see in this passage, the Lord detests those who practice the occult. In fact, He said that He would drive them out from among the people. "Witchcraft" would include even white witchcraft. It is all detestable to God. Obviously we want to avoid things that would make us detestable to God.

BUT IS ASTROLOGY ALL RIGHT?

Not unlike the tea-leaf-reading incident described earlier, in an astrology column, we could read that for our particular sign, we should not make a major decision that day. Even though there may be a significant decision God wants us to make, some Christians would not make it because of what the astrology column said. Similarly, the horoscope column might say we would meet a stranger that day who would have a major influence on our life. This could become almost a self-fulfilling prophecy, as we look carefully at every stranger that we meet wondering, "Is this the one?"

The Bible also lumps astrologers in with the sorcerers:

> 2   Then the king commanded to call the magicians, and the astrologers, and the sorcerers, and the Chaldeans, for to shew the king his dreams. So they came and stood before the king. . . .
>
> 27   Daniel answered in the presence of the king, and said, The secret which the king hath demanded cannot the wise men, the astrologers, the magicians, the soothsayers, shew unto the king;
>
> 28   But there is a God in heaven that revealeth secrets, and maketh known to the king Nebuchadnezzar what shall be in the latter days. Thy dream, and the visions of thy head upon thy bed, are these; . . .
>
> —Daniel 2, KJV

Since the Bible warns against astrology, even a casual reading of the astrology column in the newspaper would be off limits. It will influence your thinking and, thus, your behavior.

Up until this point, you may have had a different opinion about some of these practices.

Perhaps you considered that reading the astrology column in the newspaper or letting your children play with an Ouija board was harmless enough, but that is not God's opinion. We see that the occult is detestable to the Lord. Allowing your actions to be controlled by something other than God and His will is displeasing to Him. Believe it or not, *it's in the Bible!*

6

SEA MONSTERS AND DRAGONS

If you ask most Christians whether they believe what the Bible says is true, their answer would be "yes." If you then ask them whether they believe that sea monsters and dragons exist, or at least existed within recorded history, many of them would answer "no." As you will see in this chapter, this is an inconsistency. Back in Genesis, when the days of creation were being described, we find this:

> 21 And God created the great sea monsters, and every living creature that moves, with which the waters swarmed after their kind, and every winged bird after its kind; and God saw that it was good.
>
> —Genesis 1

In Psalms, we find sea monsters being commanded to praise the Lord and we also see God breaking the heads of the sea monsters:

> 7 Praise the Lord from the earth,
> Sea monsters and all deeps; . . .
>
> —Psalm 148

> 13 Thou didst divide the sea by Thy strength;
> Thou didst break the heads of the sea
> monsters in the waters.
>
> —Psalm 74

The *King James Version* of the Bible calls these *"dragons,"* in the verses we just read. Lest someone be confused and think that God is possibly talking about whales, we see a better description over in the book written by Isaiah the prophet:

> 1   In that day the Lord will punish
>   Leviathan the fleeing serpent,
>   With His fierce and great and mighty
>   sword,
>   Even Leviathan the twisted serpent;
>   And He will kill the dragon who lives in
>   the sea.
>   —Isaiah 27

Here we see that this great sea monster is a twisted serpent who lives in the sea. He is also called a dragon. One interesting thing is that this particular sea monster is given a name, Leviathan. From Psalms we know that Leviathan had more than one head:

> 14   Thou didst crush the heads of Levia-
>   than;
>   Thou didst give him as food for the
>   creatures of the wilderness.
>   —Psalm 74

From other sources, tradition has it that Leviathan had three heads. Although the Psalmist here does not tell exactly how many heads this creature had, we know that it had more than one.

Elsewhere, the book of Psalms tells us that God created Leviathan and that he has sport in the ocean:

> 24   O Lord, how many are Thy works!
>   In wisdom Thou hast made them all;
>   The earth is full of Thy possessions.
> 25   There is the sea, great and broad,
>   In which are swarms without number,
>   Animals both small and great.

26 There the ships move along,
And Leviathan, which Thou has formed
to sport in it.

—Psalm 104

In the book of Job, we find out how powerful
Leviathan is, the multi-headed dragon-serpent. God
is telling Job that only He can handle Leviathan.
He says this:

1 "Can you draw out Leviathan with a
fishhook?
Or press down his tongue with a cord?
2 "Can you put a rope in his nose?
Or pierce his jaw with a hook?
3 "Will he make many supplications to you?
Or will he speak to you soft words?
4 "Will he make a covenant with you?
Will you take him for a servant forever?
5 "Will you play with him as with a bird?
Or will you bind him for your maidens?
6 "Will the traders bargain over him?
Will they divide him among the merchants?
7 "Can you fill his skin with harpoons,
Or his head with fishing spears?
8 "Lay your hand on him;
Remember the battle; you will not do it
again!
9 "Behold, your expectation is false;
Will you be laid low even at the sight
of him?
10 "No one is so fierce that he dares to
arouse him;
Who then is he that can stand before
Me?
11 "Who has given to Me that I should repay him?
Whatever is under the whole heaven is
Mine.

12   "I will not keep silence concerning his
        limbs,
     Or his mighty strength, or his orderly
        frame.
13   "Who can strip off his outer armor?
     Who can come within his double mail?
14   "Who can open the doors of his face?
     Around his teeth there is terror.
15   "His strong scales are his pride,
     Shut up as with a tight seal.
16   "One is so near to another,
     That no air can come between them.
17   "They are joined one to another;
     They clasp each other and cannot be
        separated.
18   "His sneezes flash forth light,
     And his eyes are like the eyelids of the
        morning.
19   "Out of his mouth go burning torches;
     Sparks of fire leap forth.
20   "Out of his nostrils smoke goes forth,
     As from a boiling pot and burning
        rushes.
21   "His breath kindles coals,
     And a flame goes forth from his mouth.
22   "In his neck lodges strength,
     And dismay leaps before him.
23   "The folds of his flesh are joined to-
        gether,
     Firm on him and immovable.
24   "His heart is as hard as a stone;
     Even as hard as a lower millstone.
25   "When he raises himself up, the mighty
        fear;
     Because of the crashing they are bewil-
        dered.
26   "The sword that reaches him cannot
        avail;
     Nor the spear, the dart, or the javelin.

27 "He regards iron as straw,
    Bronze as rotten wood.
28 "The arrow cannot make him flee;
    Slingstones are turned into stubble for
        him.
29 "Clubs are regarded as stubble;
    He laughs at the rattling of the javelin.
30 "His underparts are like sharp
        potsherds;
    He spreads out like a threshing sledge
        on the mire.
31 "He makes the depths boil like a pot;
    He makes the sea like a jar of
        ointment.
32 "Behind him he makes a wake to shine;
    One would think the deep to be gray-
        haired.
33 "Nothing on earth is like him,
    One made without fear.
34 "He looks on everything that is high;
    He is king over all the sons of pride."
                                    —Job 41

    Some additional things are disclosed here about
Leviathan: out of his mouth go burning torches and
out of his nostrils smoke goes forth (verses 19 and
20). This is God Himself describing something that
He created.
    Leviathan, dragons and sea monsters may all
be extinct by now or they may not be. However,
what we do know from the Bible is that God
created them and they still existed in the time of
David and in the time of Isaiah. Please do not
regard me as a person who has gone off the deep
end. If you believe the Bible, you are forced to
believe these things also, because they are in the
Bible.
    We dismiss knights going out to fight dragons
as pure fantasy. However, we need to realize that

much of the folklore passed down has its ultimate basis in reality.

DID UNICORNS EVER EXIST?

According to the *King James* translation of the Bible, unicorns did exist at one time.   The modern translations use the term *"wild ox."* The truth is that the Hebrew word (re'em) is evidently the name of an animal that is unknown to us. From the *King James Version,* we can see why it was believed to have only one, horn:

10 But my horn shalt thou exalt like the horn of an unicorn: I shall be anointed with fresh oil.

—Psalm 92, KJV

There are numerous other places in the *King James Version* that mention unicorns:

22 God brought them out of Egypt; he hath as it were the strength of an unicorn.

—Numbers 23, KJV

8 God brought him forth out of Egypt; he hath as it were the strength of an unicorn: he shall eat up the nations his enemies, and shall break their bones, and pierce them through with his arrows.

—Numbers 24, KJV

9 Will the unicorn be willing to serve thee, or abide by thy crib?
10 Canst thou bind the unicorn with his band in the furrow? or will he harrow the valleys after thee?

—Job 39, KJV

21 Save me from the lion's mouth: for thou hast heard me from the horns of the unicorns.
—Psalm 22, KJV

17 His glory is like the firstling of his bullock, and his horns are like the horns of unicorns: with them he shall push the people together to the ends of the earth: and they are the ten thousands of Ephraim and they are the thousands of Manasseh.
—Deuteronomy 33, KJV

6 He maketh them also to skip like a calf; Lebanon and Sirion like a young unicorn.
—Psalm 29, KJV

7 And the unicorns shall come down with them, and the bullocks with the bulls; and their land shall be soaked with blood, and their dust made fat with fatness.
—Isaiah 34, KJV

It really does not matter whether or not the "re'em" was a unicorn as we envision it. What we are discovering in this chapter is that God created various unusual creatures. The mere fact that they are not around today does not mean that they never existed.

We know from fossil history that dinasours and an incredible amount of both animal and vegetable life existed on the earth in ages past, which no longer exist today. The tremendous variety that we find in the fossil record is fascinating. The mere fact that dragons, sea monsters, and unicorns do not exist in the fossil record does not mean that they never existed nor that God did not create them.

Certainly God had the creative power and imagination to create an infinite variety, all living harmoniously together. It is possible that in eternity, we will see the most magnificent of all of God's creations, creatures and plants that we could not even begin to imagine. One exciting verse in the Bible says this:

> 9 But as it is written, eye hath not seen, nor ear heard, neither have entered into the heart of man, the things which God hath prepared for them that love him.
>
> —1 Corinthians 1, KJV

In this verse, we see that these wonderful, unimaginable things that God is going to create are only for those who love God. He loves you and He wants you to enjoy those fantastic future creations. That is why He desires so earnestly to have each man, woman, boy and girl to come into a right relationship with Himself. He wants you to enjoy those things for eternity with Him.

Now let us turn our attention to man, the highest of God's creatures, and see some unusual things about him. We will look at some things that man himself decided to do, as well as considering things that God commanded him to do.

7

NUDITY AND LUST

When God created Adam and Eve, they were created naked, and they lived that way until after the fall—until after they sinned. We do not know how long they lived in the garden before they sinned and fell. For all we know, it could have been thousands of years. (Genesis says that Adam lived eight hundred years after Seth was born, but the Bible does not say how long he had lived before then.) We dealt with this somewhat in the chapter on the "Knowledge of Good and Evil." Let's see specifically what happened:

> 7 Then the eyes of both of them were opened, and they knew that they were naked; and they sewed fig leaves together and made themselves loin coverings.
> 8 And they heard the sound of the Lord God walking in the garden in the cool of the day, and the man and his wife hid themselves from the presence of the Lord God among the trees of the Garden.
> 9 Then the Lord God called to the man, and said to him, "Where are you?"
> 10 And he said, "I heard the sound of Thee in the garden, and I was afraid because I was naked; so I hid myself."

11 And He said, "Who told you that you were naked?   Have you eaten from the tree of which I commanded you not to eat?" . . .

22 Then the Lord God said, "Behold, the man has become like one of Us, knowing good and evil; and now, lest he stretch out his hand, and take also from the tree of life, and eat, and live forever"—

23 therefore the Lord God sent him out from the garden of Eden, to cultivate the ground from which he was taken.

—Genesis 3

Adam and Eve had evidently been living nude. There was nothing wrong with that, since God certainly did not consider it to be sin. After they ate of the tree of the knowledge and good and evil, they themselves concluded that being naked was wrong. Therefore they made clothes for themselves. It is interesting to note that God never said nudity was wrong. That was their own conclusion.

Following this a step further, we find that God commanded Isaiah the prophet to go naked for three years:

1 In the year that the commander came to Ashdod, when Sargon the king of Assyria sent him and he fought against Ashdod and captured it,

2 at that time the Lord spoke through Isaiah the son of Amoz, saying, "Go and loosen the sackcloth from your hips, and take your shoes off your feet."   And he did so, going naked and barefoot.

3 And the Lord said, "Even as My servant Isaiah has gone naked and barefoot three years as a sign and token against Egypt and Cush,

4 so the king of Assyria will lead away the captives of Egypt and the exiles of Cush,

young and old, naked and barefoot with buttocks uncovered, to the shame of Egypt.

—Isaiah 20

Some might think that God wanted Isaiah to
go around in just his underwear, but verse 4 makes
it absolutely clear that his buttocks were uncovered.
So Isaiah went around totally nude—without even
shoes on—for three years, because God commanded
him to do this. We know that God would not
command anyone to sin. Therefore, we can draw
the conclusion that nudity is not a sin in God's
eyes. At least it was not a sin for Isaiah; it could
be for someone else.

King Saul and the prophet Micah also were
nude at times when doing God's work:

24 And he also stripped off his clothes, and
he too prophesied before Samuel and lay down
naked all that day and all that night.
Therefore they say, "Is Saul also among the
prophets?"

—1 Samuel 19

8 Because of this I must lament and wail,
I must go barefoot and naked;
I must make a lament like the jackals
And a mourning like the ostriches.

—Micah 1

There is a difference between being nude and
being naked, just as there is a difference between
being alone and being lonely. Being unclothed,
when it is under God's command or within His will,
is not a shameful thing. However, being stripped
naked can be a shameful thing. If poor people are
naked, we are commanded to clothe them (Isaiah
58:7).

Just as an aside, the phrase "uncover the
nakedness" in the Bible is a term for having

intercourse. It is not referring to nudity. We find this numerous places, such as the following:

> 18 'And you shall not marry a woman in addition to her sister as a rival while she is alive, to uncover her nakedness.
> 19 'Also you shall not approach a woman to uncover her nakedness during her menstrual impurity. . . .'

—Leviticus 18

> 8 'You shall not uncover the nakedness of your father's wife; it is your father's nakedness.
> 9 'The nakedness of your sister, either your father's daughter or your mother's daughter, whether born at home or born outside, their nakedness you shall not uncover.
> 10 'The nakednesss of your son's daughter or your daughter's daughter, their nakedness you shall not uncover; for their nakedness is yours.
> 11 'The nakedness of your father's wife's daughter, born to your father, she is your sister, you shall not uncover her nakedness. . . .'

—Leviticus 18

We are *not* dealing here with "uncovering nakedness," which is a different subject. What we are dealing with in this chapter is nudity totally apart from lust or sex. This would include nudity, such as found in the statue of David or a painting in our national art gallery of "The Three Muses."

Even though nudity is not a sin, the Bible clearly says that sexual lust is a sin. A glamorous, young, female movie star could walk into a room wearing a gunnysack and men could lust after her. An old, fat, wrinkled woman could walk into that same room with her clothes off and the same men would likely have no lust whatsoever.

It seems to me that the main problem with nudity is that it could create lust. If it did create lust, then nudity would be wrong. By the same token, wearing skimpy or sexy clothing, if it creates lust, would be equally as wrong. In fact, skimpy and sexy clothing can sometimes create far more lust than total nudity would. It is easy to preach or speak out against nudity. However, what we should be preaching against is lust. Perhaps the reason that some preachers don't preach against lust as sin is that they might lose half of their congregation.

Lest you misunderstand, I am not advocating everyone taking off his clothes, joining a nudist colony or anything like that. It is just that I cannot find any command in Scriptures that says, "Thou shall not go nude." On the other hand, I do find a Scripture where God commanded one of his prophets to go nude. Since God commanded it, nudity must not be, in and of itself, inherently sinful.

NUDE IN FRONT OF WHOM, FOR WHAT REASON

Obviously, at times during our lives, people are going to see us without our clothes on. The real question is whether it is ever sin and, if so, when. Since the Bible is silent, man would have to make up his own rules, which could become very complicated.

Most of us have showered with members of the same sex after P.E. class in junior high and high school, or after playing a football game and such. Therefore, let's exclude being nude in front of members of the same sex as possibly being sin (at least for heterosexuals).

If we conclude that it is a sin to be nude in front of a member of the opposite sex, we run into difficulty in trying to devise our own law. For example, at what age should a mother stop bathing her son? When he is a tiny infant, it is evidently not sin. But at some point along the way, in some people's thinking, it must begin to be sin. Let us say that occurred when he was ten years old. Does this mean that it was not a sin when he was nine years, eleven months and thirty days old, and then the next day it became sin? The reason that it is stopped at a certain point is usually to avoid potential lust in the future, not because the act of being nude suddenly became sin.

Another example would be a man's aged mother who was sick and totally bedridden. Let's say she needed a bath. Would it be sin for him to give her a bath?

Another question would arise as to whether we should have only women gynecologists. Certainly a male gynecologist not only sees a woman nude, but also touches her in a very intimate way.

What about the women whom the Nazis rounded up to take to concentration camps, who were forced to strip in front of their male guards? Were all of these women sinning?

In my early days, on my grandfather's farm and my great-uncle's farm, they had "three-holer" outhouses. If you had to go, it did not matter who was in there—male or female, old or young— you simply went in and joined them. In the early days in America, and most likely in biblical days as well, there was simply a one-room cabin. People took Saturday night baths while other people were in the room. There was nudity, but no lust.

When I was fifty-four I was in the hospital with a heart attack. Then nurses gave me baths. Again, there was nudity, but no lust involved.

NUDITY AROUND THE WORLD

Many people in Third World countries, who do not have indoor plumbing, bathe publicly in the rivers. This is common in Latin America, Africa, India and on some islands in the Carribbean.

In the ancient days of Japan, there was very little heat in some of the smaller villages. In the winter, after working all day, everyone would take off their clothes and get into the public bath. They would begin to add hot rocks from a fire which heated the water. In fact, it was a challenge to see who could stay in the very longest, as the water got progressively hotter.

In the movie, "Teahouse of the August Moon," the Okinawan philosopher said that on Okinawa it was all right to see a nude lady, but it was very improper to have picture or statue of a nude lady. In America, it was okay to have picture and statue of a nude lady in a park or art museum, but was very improper to see a nude lady. This was confusing to him.

There is a tribe, which lives on the island of West Kalimantan (formerly Dutch Borneo), who go nude because of the extreme heat. They go to church this way, and there are actually pictures of them taking communion (the Lord's supper) with the entire church nude.

To most Christians in America a nude communion scene would seem terrible. However, to Christians in other parts of the world, it would seem very normal and natural. It is a very difficult task to sort out in our minds what has come from our culture, our environment and our upbringing, and what is truly part of God's character. The thing that we need to be very careful of is not to create God in our own cultural image. We need to guard against attributing characteristics to Him based on the taboos of our society. The very worst thing is to take a false image of God that we have created and to try to impose this "god" on other cultures. Often missionaries have equated Western culture with Christianity, such as the first missionaries to Hawaii. What we need to do is to introduce people to the real God of the Bible. If there are any modifications to their culture that need to be made, you can believe that God will take care of it.

In this chapter, we are not talking about pornography. There are federal laws defining pornography and prohibiting it. I think those laws should be first strictly enforced and then tightened. Child pornography and abusive sex are abominations. Bestiality, a practice depicted in some pornographic magazines, is strictly forbidden in the Bible:

> 15 'If there is a man who lies with an animal, he shall surely be put to death; you shall also kill the animal.
> 16 'If there is a woman who approaches any animal to mate with it, you shall kill the woman and the animal; they shall surely be put to death. Their bloodguiltiness is upon them.'
>
> —Leviticus 20

Let me repeat once more: God wants us to be pure and clean, morally and sexually. He does not even want lust in our hearts, much less in our activities. But we cannot jump from that to a condemnation of all nudity. It occurs today in some circumstances and has through the centuries, at times even at God's command.

In no way am I advocating nudity. I am advocating a realistic view of God, the God who commanded one of His prophets to go nude for three years. Does your God condemn all nudity?

8

FORNICATION

Fornication is condemned by God and it is sin. However, I have heard many preachers say that adultery is sex between a married person and someone else, and fornication is sex between two single people. That simply does not square with the Bible's definition of fornication.

As we will see, fornication is a broad term for sexual misconduct, sexual abuse, and sexual immorality. Adultery is simply one form of fornication. A husband and wife can commit fornication with each other, if one is sexually abusing or taking advantage of the other.

The word fornication is most frequently used in connection with having sex with a harlot:

1 And there came one of the seven angels which had the seven vials, and talked with me, saying unto me, Come hither; I will shew unto thee the judgment of the great whore that sitteth upon many waters:
2 With whom the kings of the earth have committed fornication, and the inhabitants of the earth have been made drunk with the wine of her fornication.

—Revelation 17, KJV

3 For all nations have drunk of the wine
of the wrath of her fornication, and the kings
of the earth have committed fornication with
her, and the merchants of the earth are waxed
rich through the abundance of her delicacies.
—Revelation 18, KJV

One place where we see that fornication is a
broad term that includes adultery is in Paul's letter
to the Corinthians:

1 It is reported commonly that there is
fornication among you, and such fornication as
is not so much as named among the Gentiles,
that one should have his father's wife.
—1 Corinthians 5, KJV

Here we see that someone having his father's
wife (who was married), is described as fornication.
This could either be his mother or his stepmother.
Apparently this was considered so gross, that it was
referred to by the broader term of fornication.

Other passages which further indicate that
fornication is not merely sex between two single
people, but can also be committed by a married
person, is when Jesus talked about putting away a
wife:

31 It hath been said, Whosoever shall put
away his wife, let him give her a writing of
divorcement:
32 But I say unto you, That whosoever
shall put away his wife, saving for the cause
of fornication, causeth her to commit adultery:
and whosoever shall marry her that is divorced
committeth adultery.
—Matthew 5, KJV

9 And I say unto you, Whosoever shall put
away his wife, except it be for fornication,

and shall marry another, committeth adultery:
and whoso marrieth her which is put away
doth commit adultery.

—Matthew 19, KJV

The preceding verse says that a wife can
commit fornication (it does not say adultery). If
she does, her husband can put her away.

I am in no way condoning sex between two
single people. I am merely pointing out that this is
not what the word fornication means. I believe
single people should keep themselves pure and hold
themselves sexually in reserve for whomever they
are going to marry. This is particularly true with
the AIDS plague running rampant. In the future,
virginity is going to be at a high premium, and it
pleases God.

SEX BETWEEN SINGLE PEOPLE

In the Bible, if a girl was not a virgin when
she got married, she was stoned to death. That is
how strongly God was against premarital sex:

13 "If any man takes a wife and goes in to
her and then turns against her,
14 and charges her with shameful deeds and
publicly defames her, and says, 'I took this
woman, but when I came near her, I did not
find her a virgin,'
15 then the girl's father and mother shall
take and bring out the evidence of the girl's
virginity to the elders of the city at the gate.
16 "And the girl's father shall say to the
elders, 'I gave my daughter to this man for a
wife, but he turned against her;
17 and behold, he has charged her with
shameful deeds, saying, "I did not find your
daughter a virgin." But this is the evidence of

my daughter's virginity.' And they shall spread the garment before the elders of the city.

18 "So the elders of the city shall take the man and chastise him,

19 and they shall fine him a hundred shekels of silver and give it to the girl's father, because he publicly defamed a virgin of Israel. And she shall remain his wife; he cannot divorce her all his days.

20 "But if this charge is true, that the girl was not found a virgin,

21 then they shall bring out the girl to the doorway of her father's house, and the men of her city shall stone her to death because she has committed an act of folly in Israel, by playing the harlot in her father's house; thus you shall purge the evil from among you. . . ."

—Deuteronomy 22

Another way we know that God was against premarital sex is that any illegitimate offspring was condemned until the tenth generation, and could not even enter the assembly of the Lord:

2 A bastard shall not enter into the congregation of the Lord; even to his tenth generation shall he not enter into the congregation of the Lord.

—Deuteronomy 23, KJV

While we are considering sex as it relates to the single person, it is interesting to note that masturbation is never mentioned in the Bible. The Bible is totally silent on the subject. A widely-recognized Christian expert on the family feels that if there is no lust involved, then masturbation is okay. I would certainly bow to his wisdom in this matter. One thing I do know is that we cannot arbitrarily attribute a characteristic to God that He is against masturbation, since the Bible never mentions the subject.

Even though fornication does not simply mean sex between single people, God is apparently against it.

ABSTAIN FROM FORNICATION

It is God's will that we avoid fornication and abstain from it, whether it be adultery, or any other form:

3 For this is the will of God, even your sanctification, that ye should abstain from fornication:

—1 Thessalonians 4, KJV

18 Flee fornication. Every sin that a man doeth is without the body; but he that committeth fornication sinneth against his own body.

19 What? know ye not that your body is the temple of the Holy Ghost which is in you, which ye have of God, and ye are not your own?

20 For ye are bought with a price: therefore glorify God in your body, and in your spirit, which are God's.

—1 Corinthians 6, KJV

13 Meats for the belly, and the belly for meats: but God shall destroy both it and them. Now the body is not for fornication, but for the Lord; and the Lord for the body.

—1 Corinthians 6, KJV

We are warned not to give in to the lusts of the flesh and, if we do, these are some of the things that will occur, according to Saint Paul:

19 Now the works of the flesh are manifest, which are these; Adultery, fornication, uncleanness, lasciviousness,

20 Idolatry, witchcraft, hatred, variance, emulations, wrath, strife, seditions, heresies,

21 Envyings, murders, drunkenness, revellings, and such like: of the which I tell you before, as I have also told you in time past, that they which do such things shall not inherit the kingdom of God.

—Galatians 5, KJV

You will notice that if one is involved in doing the things listed in these verses, verse 21 tells us that such a person will not inherit the kingdom of God. That list includes fornication.

In the next few chapters, we will examine some different sexual relationships, most of which are not fornication, as we will see.

9

PERMANENT MISTRESSES

In the Bible, the word "concubine" is used a great deal. Some might think of concubines as second-class wives, although they are never called wives. Really a concubine is a permanent mistress. The children of concubines could not share in the inheritance along with the children of the wives. However, evidently the men had sexual relations with their concubines which resulted in children.

> 6 but to the sons of his concubines, Abraham gave gifts while he was still living, and sent them away from his son Isaac eastward, to the land of the east.
>
> —Genesis 25

> 12 And Timna was a concubine of Esau's son Eliphaz and she bore Amalek to Eliphaz. These are the sons of Esau's wife Adah.
>
> —Genesis 36

CAPTIVE WOMEN

There is a strange story in the Old Testament that typifies what happened after many of the battles and conquests of the children of Israel. The menfolk of the enemy were killed, but the virgin girls were passed out among the men of Israel:

1 Then the Lord spoke to Moses, saying,

2 "Take full vengeance for the sons of Israel on the Midianites; afterward you will be gathered to your people."

3 And Moses spoke to the people, saying, "Arm men from among you for the war, that they may go against Midian, to execute the Lord's vengeance on Midian.

4 "A thousand from each tribe of all the tribes of Israel you shall send to the war."

5 So there were furnished from the thousands of Israel, a thousand from each tribe, twelve thousand armed for war.

6 And Moses sent them, a thousand from each tribe, to the war, and Phinehas the son of Eleazar the priest, to the war with them, and the holy vessels and the trumpets for the alarm in his hand.

7 So they made war against Midian, just as the Lord had commanded Moses, and they killed every male.

8 And they killed the kings of Midian along with the rest of their slain: Evi and Rekem and Zur and Hur and Reba, the five kings of Midian; they also killed Balaam the son of Beor with the sword.

9 And the sons of Israel captured the women of Midian and their little ones; and all their cattle and all their flocks and all their goods, they plundered.

10 Then they burned all their cities where they lived and all their camps with fire.

11 And they took all the spoil and all the prey, both of man and of beast.

12 And they brought the captives and the prey and the spoil to Moses, and to Eleazar the priest and to the congregation of the sons

of Israel, to the camp at the plains of Moab,
which are by the Jordan opposite Jericho.

13 And Moses and Eleazar the priest and
all the leaders of the congregation went out to
meet them outside the camp.

14 And Moses was angry with the officers
of the army, the captains of thousands and the
captains of hundreds, who had come from
service in the war.

15 And Moses said to them, "Have you
spared all the women?

16 "Behold, these caused the sons of Israel,
through the counsel of Balaam, to trespass
against the Lord in the matter of Peor, so the
plague was among the congregation of the
Lord.

17 "Now therefore, kill every male among
the little ones, and kill every woman who has
known man intimately.

18 "But all the girls who have not known
man intimately, spare for yourselves. . . ."

—Numbers 31

In the passage above, we see that all of the
men were killed, including male babies just a few
days old. In addition, all the women who had had
intercourse were killed, but the virgin girls were
spared for the menfolk. In this particular case,
there was quite a large number of them.

32 Now the booty that remained from the
spoil which the men of war had plundered was
675,000 sheep.

33 and 72,000 cattle,

34 and 61,000 donkeys,

35 and of human beings, of the women who
had not known man intimately, all the persons
were 32,000.

—Numbers 31

The 32,000 virgin girls could have ranged in age from a few days to perhaps 18 or 19 years old, and these were given as booty to the sons of Israel.

Many of the more desirable young ladies would be taken by the men as concubines. A man would have relations with one of these virgins and she would remain in his household in a permanent, mistress-type of arrangement. However, the children that these concubines bore would not be considered heirs.

Concubines could be Hebrew women, as well as women of other races. The reason King Solomon had so many concubines is that kings of other countries would give him one or two of their daughters to be Solomon's wives or concubines, which would tend to ensure that Solomon would not attack that country. Evidently, King Solomon had a large number of these:

> **3 And he had seven hundred wives, princesses, and three hundred concubines, and his wives turned his heart away.**
>
> **—1 Kings 11**

But in this last verse, we see the danger in concubines and multiple wives. They can divert a man's attention away from where it should be. In this case, Solomon's wives and concubines turned his heart away from God.

In today's world, many men—unfortunately even Christian men—have lusted after another woman to have as a mistress and have been willing to throw away a good marriage, family, job and, in some cases, even a ministry to accomodate that lust.

DAVID AND THE TEN CONCUBINES

When David's son, Absalom, was trying to take over the kingdom from David, David had to flee

Jerusalem, but he left ten of his concubines behind to keep house:

> 16 So the king went out and all his household with him. But the king left ten concubines to keep the house.
>
> —2 Samuel 15

Counsel was given to Absalom to go to these ten concubines and have intercourse with them, so that the people of Israel would then know that he was king. Absalom took that advice:

> 21 And Ahithophel said to Absalom, "Go in to your father's concubines, whom he has left to keep the house; then all Israel will hear that you have made yourself odious to your father. The hands of all who are with you will also be strengthened."
> 22 So they pitched a tent for Absalom on the roof, and Absalom went in to his father's concubines in the sight of all Israel.
>
> —2 Samuel 16

Later, when Absalom died and David returned to Jerusalem, he would not have intercourse with those ten concubines:

> 3 Then David came to his house at Jerusalem, and the king took the ten women, the concubines whom he had left to keep the house, and placed them under guard and provided them with sustenance, but did not go in to them. So they were shut up until the day of their death, living as widows.
>
> —2 Samuel 20

So we see that David stopped having the normal sexual relationship of a man with his concubine with these ten women. He continued to provide for them, but he kept them shut up and living as widows until their death.

THE TWELVE SONS OF JACOB

The twelve sons of Jacob (Israel) were the heads of the twelve tribes of Israel. Jacob had two wives, Leah and Rachel. Do you think that all twelve of his sons were borne by his two wives? Many people assume so. Actually, only eight of his sons were borne by his two wives:

> **22 And it came about while Israel was dwelling in that land, that Reuben went and lay with Bilhah his father's concubine; and Israel heard of it.**
> **Now there were twelve sons of Jacob—**
> **23 the sons of Leah: Reuben, Jacob's first-born, then Simeon and Levi and Judah and Issachar and Zebulun;**
> **24 the sons of Rachel: Joseph and Benjamin;**
> **25 and the sons of Bilhah, Rachel's maid: Dan and Naphtali;**
> **26 and the sons of Zilpah, Leah's maid: Gad and Asher. These are the sons of Jacob who were born to him in Paddanaram.**
> **27 And Jacob came to his father Isaac at Mamre of Kiriath-arba (that is, Hebron), where Abraham and Isaac had sojourned.**
> **—Genesis 35**

Four of the heads of the tribes were sons of Jacob's concubines. Verse 22 of the preceding passage says that Bilhah was his concubine, and verse 25 says that she was Rachel's maid. Thus, as Jacob had relations with his concubines, the resulting four male offspring became heads of four of the tribes of Israel. So God blessed the sexual relationship between Jacob and his mistresses (concubines). Genesis 30 also verifies that Bilhah,

Rachel's maid, was in the relationship of a concubine to Jacob, and she bore him children:

> 1 Now when Rachel saw that she bore Jacob no children, she became jealous of her sister; and she said to Jacob, "Give me children, or else I die."
>
> 2 Then Jacob's anger burned against Rachel, and he said, "Am I in the place of God, who has withheld from you the fruit of the womb?"
>
> 3 And she said, "Here is my maid Bilhah, go in to her, that she may bear on my knees, that through her I too may have children."
>
> 4 So she gave him her maid Bilhah as a wife, and Jacob went in to her.
>
> 5 And Bilhah conceived and bore Jacob a son.
>
> 6 Then Rachel said, "God has vindicated me, and has indeed heard my voice and has given me a son." Therefore she named him Dan.
>
> 7 And Rachel's maid Bilhah conceived again and bore Jacob a second son.
>
> —Genesis 30

CONCUBINES IN OTHER COUNTRIES

This practice of having concubines was not limited to the children of Israel. When Belshazzar, king of Babylon, was having the big feast whereat ultimately God's hand wrote on the wall, he had the golden vessels from the temple of Jerusalem brought out, and he, his wives and his concubines drank from them:

> 3 Then they brought the gold vessels that had been taken out of the temple, the house of God which was in Jerusalem; and the king

and his nobles, his wives, and his concubines
drank from them.

—Daniel 5

When did this practice of having concubines
cease? Was it sometime prior to the time of Christ
or was it sometime afterward? The Bible does not
tell us. Christ never said a word about concubines,
so either the practice had ceased by then, or it was
a practice that He did not condemn.

In some ways, this practice of having "concubines" has continued on into our modern era.
Some of the plantation owners in the south, during
the time of slavery, would take a beautiful black
girl in a concubine-type relationship. The result
was mulatto offspring. In South Africa, a similar
situation occurred, and the "coloreds" (a mixed race
between blacks and whites) today represent quite a
large population there. So, evidently there were
many who had this concubine relationship in the
earlier days in South Africa.

RESPONSIBILITY TO CARE FOR CONCUBINES

When you consider the fact that thousands of
men were killed off in wars, you realize that there
was likely a very disproportionate ratio between
men and women. If the Israelites killed off all of
the men in some of the nations that they conquered
but kept alive the virgin females, that would have
further increased the ratio of women to men.
Given that women were not free agents in the sense
that they are in today's world, it becomes easier to
understand this concubine system that seemed to be
perfectly acceptable at the time. Someone would
have to care for all of these women. In Judges, we
see this as one of the results of the frequent wars:

30 'Are they not finding, are they not di-
viding the spoil?

A maiden, two maidens for every warrior; . . .'

—Judges 5

Interestingly, in biblical practice, one did not
take on concubines simply for the sake of having
more sexual "conquests"—as some may practice
today.   Rather, there was a responsibility on the
part of the man to care for those concubines and
to provide for their needs for the remainder of
their lives.   As we saw in the example with David,
when his son Absolom violated his ten concubines,
even though he did not have further sexual relations with them after that incident, David still felt
an obligation to provide for them for the duration
of their lifetime.

So we see that these practices, though very
different from our modern, western society, had an
order and responsibility to them.

Jesus certainly did not advocate any type of
immorality or promiscuous sexual behavior, nor do I.
I am simply reporting a practice that occurred
during biblical days, without it ever being condemned.   God must not be as much of a prude as
some of us are.   Whether we like it or not, *it is in
the Bible.*

10

MULTIPLE WIVES

Once a missionary in Africa led a tribal chief to a saving knowledge of Jesus Christ. This tribal chief had had two wives for many years, and they were all three in their fifties and sixties. The tribal chief, being a new Christian, was neither an elder nor leader in the church, yet the missionary told him that he could not be baptized and would not really be a Christian, unless he sent away one of his wives. He was told that he had to choose which one he would keep and which one he would put away.

I read the story of what happened when he finally had to choose. He gave the wife he had chosen to be sent away one final hug, as all three of them had tears running down their faces. She went out into the night and ultimately wandered off into the desert and died, because she had no desire to live apart from the husband she had known for some thirty years.

I cannot find in the Scriptures any basis for the missionary requiring that of the tribal chief. Jesus Himself must have encountered men who had more than one wife. There is no record of Him telling them to get rid of one. In no way is this an attempt to justify or to recommend the old Mormon tradition of multiple wives. In the first place, it is illegal in America, and the Bible tells us to obey the laws of the land. We are simply looking at what the Bible has to say on this subject.

As one reads through the Old Testament, it is interesting to observe that almost every one of the patriarchs had multiple wives. In fact, David had at least seven wives, in addition to his concubines. In looking at concubines in the last chapter, we saw that they were essentially permanent, legal mistresses.

Here is what the Bible says about David and his wives, in listing his offspring:

1   Now these were the sons of David who were born to him in Hebron: the first-born was Amnon, by Ahinoam the Jezreelitess; the second was Daniel, by Abigail the Carmelitess;

2   the third was Absalom the son of Maacah, the daughter of Talmai king of Geshur; the forth was Adonijah the son of Haggith;

3   the fifth was Shephatiah, by Abital; the sixth was Ithream, by his wife Eglah.

4   Six were born to him in Hebron, and there he reigned seven years and six months. And in Jerusalem he reigned thirty-three years.

5   And these were born to him in Jerusalem: Shimea, Shobab, Nathan, and Solomon, four, by Bath-shua the daughter of Ammiel;

6   and Ibhar, Elishama, Eliphelet,

7   Nogah, Nepheg, and Japhia,

8   Elishama, Eliada, and Eliphelet, nine.

9   All these were the sons of David, besides the sons of the concubines; and Tamar was their sister.

—1 Chronicles 3

The Bible clearly states that David was a man after God's own heart (Acts 13:22). Certainly, if God had considered having multiple wives a sin,

David would not have been considered "a man after God's own heart." So we see that this practice did not prevent him from being a godly man—a man after God's own heart.

Most people are familiar with Abraham. They know that he had two sons, Isaac and Ishmael, who were born to him by Sarah and her maid, Hagar. If you asked people, "How many sons did Abraham have?" the majority would answer, "two." Wrong. Most people do not realize that Abraham had a total of eight sons and he took a third wife:

> 1 Now Abraham took another wife, whose name was Keturah.
> 2 And she bore to him Zimran and Jokshan and Medan and Midian and Ishbak and Shuah.
> —Genesis 25

Abraham also had concubines (mistresses), who also gave him sons:

> 5 Now Abraham gave all that he had to Isaac;
> 6 but to the sons of his concubines, Abraham gave gifts while he was still living, and sent them away from his son Isaac eastward, to the land of the east.
> —Genesis 25

Rehoboam, the son of Solomon, was king after Solomon. The Bible says that he had eighteen wives and sixty permanent mistresses (concubines):

> 17 And they strengthened the kingdom of Judah and supported Rehoboam the son of Solomon for three years, for they walked in the way of David and Solomon for three years.
> 18 Then Rehoboam took as a wife Mahalath the daughter of Jerimoth the son of David and

of Abihail the daughter of Eliab the son of Jesse,

19 and she bore him sons: Jeush, Shemariah, and Zaham.

20 And after her he took Maacah the daughter of Absalom, and she bore him Abijah, Attai, Ziza, and Shelomith.

21 And Rehoboam loved Maacah the daughter of Absalom more than all his other wives and concubines. For he had taken eighteen wives and sixty concubines and fathered twenty-eight sons and sixty daughters.

22 And Rehoboam appointed Abijah the son of Maacah as head and leader among his brothers, for he intended to make him king.

23 And he acted wisely and distributed some of his sons through all the territories of Judah and Benjamin to all the fortified cities, and he gave them food in abundance. And he sought many wives for them.

—2 Chronicles 11

Here we see that Solomon's son had eighteen wives, in addition to sixty concubines (mistresses) and fathered twenty-eight sons and sixty daughters. However, Solomon was the grand prize winner when it comes to the number of wives and concubines. He had seven hundred wives and three hundred concubines. In his old age, his wives turned his heart away from God, as we saw briefly in the last chapter. However, it is indicated that it was Solomon turning to worship their idols that was his sin, and not the fact that he had multiple wives:

1 Now King Solomon loved many foreign women along with the daughter of Pharaoh: Moabite, Ammonite, Edomite, Sidonian, and Hittite women,

2 from the nations concerning which the Lord had said to the sons of Israel, "You shall

not associate with them, neither shall they associate with you, for they will surely turn your heart away after their gods." Solomon held fast to these in love.

3 And he had seven hundred wives, princesses, and three hundred concubines, and his wives turned his heart away.

4 For it came about when Solomon was old, his wives turned his heart away after other gods; and his heart was not wholly devoted to the Lord his God, as the heart of David his father had been.

5 For Solomon went after Ashtoreth the goddess of the Sidonians and after Milcom the detestable idol of the Ammonites.

6 And Solomon did what was evil in the sight of the Lord, and did not follow the Lord fully, as David his father had done.

7 Then Solomon built a high place for Chemosh the detestable idol of Moab, on the mountain which is east of Jerusalem, and for Molech the detestable idol of the sons of Ammon.

8 Thus also he did for all his foreign wives, who burned incense and sacrificed to their gods.

—1 Kings 11

There is nothing whatsoever in the Old Testament that indicates a man cannot have more than one wife. In fact, the Bedouins who live in the nation of Israel today have multiple wives. Interestingly, in Bedouin custom, one cannot take on another wife, unless he can provide for her, which requires providing her own tent and certain other necessities. Again, we see the responsibility of caring for the needs of the wives as an integral part of this custom. Among the Bedouins, the more wives a man has, the richer he is, because he has more people to take care of larger flocks.

In the Bible, only if one is going to be an an elder or an overseer of a church is he limited to one wife:

1 It is a trustworthy statement: if any man aspires to the office of overseer, it is a fine work he desires to do.

2 An overseer, then, must be above reproach, the husband of one wife, temperate, prudent, respectable, hospitable, able to teach,

3 not addicted to wine or pugnacious, but gentle, uncontentious, free from the love of money.

—1 Timothy 3

Evidently, an overseer or an elder would have to spend much time looking after the affairs of the church and would not have time to worry about multiple wives. (I am not talking about a man whose wife has died, and he has since remarried, or about a divorced man who is remarried. I am viewing this passage solely as it might relate to the subject at hand—having more than one wife at the same time.) However, for any Christian other than a church elder, there is nothing I can find in the Bible that says he cannot have more than one wife at a time.

In the United States, one can only have one wife because of the laws of our land. This is true in many nations. However, there are also many nations, such as the Arab nations, wherein having more than one wife is legal according to the laws of the land. Moslims in Indonesia for example, can have four wives, but no more. If a Christian man were a citizen of such a country, and not an elder in the church, then there is nothing in the Bible that prohibits him from having more than one wife.

The danger is that this would take one's eyes and attention away from the Lord, as it did with Solomon. However, with Abraham, Jacob and many others, evidently it did not take their heart and mind away from the Lord.

MULTIPLE WIVES REQUIRED

Not only were multiple wives tolerated in the Scriptures, but they were actually required at times under certain circumstances. If a brother died having no son, the remaining brother was obligated to take the widow as a wife to himself, so that she could bear sons. The brother was obligated to do this, even if he already had one or more wives:

> 7 But Er, Judah's first-born, was evil in the sight of the Lord, so the Lord took his life.
> 8 Then Judah said to Onan, "Go in to your brother's wife, and perform your duty as a brother-in-law to her, and raise up offspring for your brother."
> 9 And Onan knew that the offspring would not be his; so it came about that when he went in to his brother's wife, he wasted his seed on the ground, in order not to give offspring to his brother.
> 10 But what he did was displeasing in the sight of the Lord; so He took his life also.
> —Genesis 38

> 5 "When brothers live together and one of them dies and has no son, the wife of the deceased shall not be married outside the family to a strange man. Her husband's brother shall go in to her and take her to himself as wife and perform the duty of a husband's brother to her.
> 6 "And it shall be that the first-born whom she bears shall assume the name of his dead brother, that his name may not be blotted out from Israel. . . ."
> —Deuteronomy 25

In the New Testament when Jesus was asked about this practice, this is what He had to say:

23 On that day some Sadducees (who say there is no resurrection) came to Him and questioned Him,

24 saying, "Teacher, Moses said, 'IF A MAN DIES, HAVING NO CHILDREN, HIS BROTHER AS NEXT OF KIN SHALL MARRY HIS WIFE, AND RAISE UP AN OFFSPRING TO HIS BROTHER.'

25 "Now there were seven brothers with us; and the first married and died, and having no offspring left his wife to his brother;

26 so also the second, and the third, down to the seventh.

27 "And last of all, the woman died.

28 "In the resurrection therefore whose wife of the seven shall she be? For they all had her."

29 But Jesus answered and said to them, "You are mistaken, not understanding the Scriptures, or the power of God.

30 "For in the resurrection they neither marry, nor are given in marriage, but are like angels in heaven.

31 "But regarding the resurrection of the dead, have you not read that which was spoken to you by God, saying,

32 "'I AM THE GOD OF ABRAHAM, AND THE GOD OF ISAAC, AND THE GOD OF JACOB'? He is not the God of the dead but of the living.

33 And when the multitudes heard this, they were astonished at His teaching.

—Matthew 22

In the answer Jesus gave, you will notice that He did not have a single word of condemnation for this practice. If it were a sinful thing or something that displeased God, it seems to me He surely would have condemned the practice.

As I mentioned in the last chapter, so many of the men would have been killed during the wars, especially the young men. This would have left a surplus of women. This would be one of the reasons that multiple wives were necessary. Rather than these women "drying up on the vine," multiple wives were allowed and, in some cases, required. It is likely that this was in order to expand the race to more rapidly to fill the land.

It was also biblical for men to marry wives from women they captured during war:

> 10 "When you go out to battle against your enemies, and the Lord your God delivers them into your hands, and you take them away captive,
>
> 11 and see among the captives a beautiful woman, and have a desire for her and would take her as a wife for yourself,
>
> 12 then you shall bring her home to your house, and she shall shave her head and trim her nails.
>
> 13 "She shall also remove the clothes of her captivity and shall remain in your house, and mourn her father and mother a full month; and after that you may go in to her and be her husband and she shall be your wife.
>
> 14 "And it shall be, if you are not pleased with her, then you shall let her go wherever she wishes; but you shall certainly not sell her for money, you shall not mistreat her, because you have humbled her. . . ."

—Deuteronomy 21

This applied even if a man already had a wife. However, there were areas wherein he could not show partiality to this new wife. The passage in Deuteronomy continues this way:

15 "If a man has two wives, the one loved and the other unloved, and both the loved and the unloved have borne him sons, if the first-born son belongs to the unloved,
16 then it shall be in the day he wills what he has to his sons, he cannot make the son of the loved the first-born before the son of the unloved who is the first-born. . . ."
—Deuteronomy 21

The Israelites practiced what we would call polygamy. Researchers today say that Americans practice polygamy, but it is "serial polygamy." We have one wife for a few years, then divorce her, have another wife for a few years, put her away, and then marry another, and so forth.

WHAT ABOUT THE COMMAND IN TIMOTHY TO HAVE ONLY ONE WIFE?

We have already noted that the only place in the Scriptures that says a man is limited to one wife is in the writings to Timothy and Titus. There are many biblical scholars who feel that the two letters to Timothy and the one to Titus were not written by Paul, and should not be contained in the New Testament. They base this on the grounds that Paul's travels described in these three letters do not fit anywhere into the historical account of the book of Acts. Also, in the book of Acts, Paul would be in a place a very short period of time, appoint elders and move on. Yet the criteria for elders found in these epistles, and the church organization described in them, is that of the second century. Also, there is vocabulary used that is not used anywhere in Paul's other letters and the style is significantly different from the other letters that Paul has written.

Whether or not the two letters to Timothy and the one to Titus should be in the New Testament is not a matter for discussion in this book. I personally think they belong in the Bible. However, if there is something in those three letters that tends to conflict or disagree with the rest of Scriptures. In such a case, I would tend to minimize the things found in the letters to Timothy and Titus.

As we have said, the only biblical restriction for having one wife is found in the first letter to Timothy and in the letter to Titus. The fact that such a restriction is found no place else in the Scriptures would bring it into some question, at least in minds of biblical scholars. There is a verse in the New Testament that talks about a man having his "own" wife (1 Corinthians 7:2), but there is nothing that restricts this to meaning just one.

As I said earlier, multiple wives are illegal in the United States and that, among other reasons, would preclude the practice here. However, we do not have a biblical basis for requiring monogamy of those who are not church leaders in other cultures. I am certainly not advocating changing the laws of the U.S. to allow multiple wives. I am for changing our view of God to a realistic one. Let us worship the God who is in the Bible.

11

MARRY A PROSTITUTE

What would you think if the wife of some major Christian leader, such as Billy Graham, were to die and Billy Graham then said that he felt God wanted him to go marry the happy hooker, Xaviera Hollander?

Most Christians would feel that Billy Graham had backslidden and was outside the will of God. Let's say that he did marry the happy hooker and they had three children. Let's further say that after awhile she abandoned Billy Graham and the three children and went back to being a prostitute, but God told Billy to go and bring her back even though she had committed adultery multiple times. Suppose Billy then took her back. Many would think that he was foolish or stupid. Yet that is exactly what God commanded one of his prophets to do:

> 2 When the Lord first spoke through Hosea, the Lord said to Hosea, "Go, take to yourself a wife of harlotry, and have children of harlotry; for the land commits flagrant harlotry, forsaking the Lord."
> 3 So he went and took Gomer the daughter of Diblaim, and she conceived and bore him a son.

4 And the Lord said to him, "Name him Jezreel; for yet a little while, and I will punish the house of Jehu for the bloodshed of Jezreel, and I will put an end to the kingdom of the house of Israel.

5 "And it will come about on that day, that I will break the bow of Israel in the valley of Jezreel."

6 Then she conceived again and gave birth to a daughter.   And the Lord said to him, "Name her Lo-ruhamah, for I will no longer have compassion on the house of Israel, that I should ever forgive them.

7 "But I will have compassion on the house of Judah and deliver them by the Lord their God, and will not deliver them by bow, sword, battle, horses, or horsemen."

8 When she had weaned Lo-ruhamah, she conceived and gave birth to a son.

9 And the Lord said, "Name him Lo-ammi, for you are not My people and I am not your God."

—Hosea 1

Then Chapter 2 records the return of Hosea's wife to her harlotry:

5 "For their mother has played the harlot;
She who conceived them has acted shamefully.
For she said, 'I will go after my lovers,
Who give me my bread and my water,
My wool and my flax, my oil and my drink.' . . ."

—Hosea 2

God then commands Hosea to go once again and buy back (redeem) his adulterous wife:

1   Then the Lord said to me, "Go again, love a woman who is loved by her husband, yet an adulteress, even as the Lord loves the sons of Israel, though they turn to other gods and love raisin cakes."

2   So I bought her for myself for fifteen shekels of silver and a homer and a half of barley.

3   Then I said to her, "You shall stay with me for many days. You shall not play the harlot, nor shall you have a man; so I will also be toward you."

4   For the sons of Israel will remain for many days without king or prince, without sacrifice or sacred pillar, and without ephod or household idols.

5   Afterward the sons of Israel will return and seek the Lord their God and David their king; and they will come trembling to the Lord and to His goodness in the last days.

—Hosea 3

God did this as a physical illustration so that all could see that, even though the children of Israel were playing the harlot and going after other gods, He would redeem them.   We know that the ultimate redemption was Jesus Christ.   How great is God's grace!

Again, I am certainly not recommending that one go marry a hooker or even that a Christian marry a non-Christian.   I am simply reporting something that God commanded one of His prophets to do. It pleased God that Hosea was obedient to him. God does not fit into our mold. What He may ask us to do may be very unusual.   We need to be sure that it is He who is asking, and then be careful to obey.

THERE IS LIFE AFTER ADULTERY

Many people today feel that if either party to a marriage commits adultery, the marriage is over. They look at adultery as the "ultimate sin" which would automatically dissolve a marriage.

However, in the case of Hosea, after his wife left him and committed adultery, God told him to redeem her and have her as his wife. So, evidently, in God's eyes, a marriage can go on after one party commits adultery. Again, don't argue with me. I am simply reporting what the Bible has to say.

12

ADULTERY

We have been using the Old Testament in some of our examples. As Christians, we are not under Old Testament law, and yet the Old Testament tells us what God is like, what pleases Him and what displeases Him. We need to study it. It was written for our benefit:

> 4 For whatever was written in earlier times was written for our instruction, that through perseverance and the encouragement of the Scriptures we might have hope.
> —Romans 15

The Bible makes it amply clear that we are not to share our wife with another man, nor are we to go in to our neighbor's wife. Solomon, the sex king of the Bible, makes this very clear. As you read this next passage, you will see that he is not talking about a water well, but about one's wife:

> 15 Drink water from your own cistern,
> And fresh water from your own well.
> 16 Should your springs be dispersed abroad,
> Streams of water in the streets?
> 17 Let them be yours alone,
> And not for strangers with you.

18 Let your fountain be blessed,
And rejoice in the wife of your youth.
19 As a loving hind and a graceful doe,
Let her breasts satisfy you at all times;
Be exhilarated always with her love.
20 For why should you, my son, be exhilarated with an adulteress,
And embrace the bosom of a foreigner?
21 For the ways of a man are before the
eyes of the Lord,
And He watches all his paths.
—Proverbs 5

The writings of Solomon warn against going in to your neighbor's wife, while Leviticus strictly prohibits it:

23 For the commandment is a lamp, and
the teaching is light;
And reproofs for discipline are the way
of life,
24 To keep you from the evil woman,
From the smooth tongue of the adulteress.
25 Do not desire her beauty in your heart,
Nor let her catch you with her eyelids.
26 For on account of a harlot one is reduced to a loaf of bread,
And an adulteress hunts for the precious
life.
27 Can a man take fire in his bosom,
And his clothes not be burned?
28 Or can a man walk on hot coals,
And his feet not be scorched?
29 So is the one who goes in to his neighbor's wife;
Whoever touches her will not go unpunished.
30 Men do not despise a thief if he steals
To satisfy himself when he is hungry;

31 But when he is found, he must repay
      sevenfold;
    He must give all the substance of his
      house.
32 The one who commits adultery with a
      woman is lacking sense;
    He who would destroy himself does it.
33 Wounds and disgrace he will find,
    And his reproach will not be blotted out.
34 For jealousy enrages a man,
    And he will not spare in the day of
      vengeance.
35 He will not accept any ransom,
    Nor will he be content though you give
      many gifts.

—Proverbs 6

20 'And you shall not have intercourse with
your neighbor's wife, to be defiled with her. . . .'

—Leviticus 18

Obviously, adultery is prohibited. We know from the story Jesus told about the good Samaritan, that our "neighbor" includes everyone (Luke 10:29-37). So, the prohibition against going in to our neighbor's wife would include all married ladies.

Solomon tells us in Proverbs 7 that the end result of adultery is death. The law specifically says that the penalty for adultery is death; that is how much God hates adultery:

1 Then the Lord spoke to Moses, saying,...

10 'If there is a man who commits adultery with another man's wife, one who commits adultery with his friend's wife, the adulterer and the adulteress shall surely be put to death.

11 If there is a man who lies with his father's wife, he has uncovered his father's nakedness; both of them shall surely be put to death, their bloodguiltiness is upon them.

24 'Then he shall make the woman drink the water of bitterness that brings a curse, so that the water which brings a curse will go into her and cause bitterness.

25 'And the priest shall take the grain offering of jealousy from the woman's hand, and he shall wave the grain offering before the Lord and bring it to the altar;

26 and the priest shall take a handful of the grain offering as its memorial offering and offer it up in smoke on the altar, and afterward he shall make the woman drink the water.

27 'When he has made her drink the water, then it shall come about, if she has defiled herself and has been unfaithful to her husband, that the water which brings a curse shall go into her and cause bitterness, and her abdomen will swell and her thigh will waste away, and the woman will become a curse among her people.

28 'But if the woman has not defiled herself and is clean, she will then be free and conceive children. . . .'

—Numbers 5

In this fairly long passage above, evidently God Himself will punish a woman guilty of having intercourse with another man while she is married. Intercouse of that type brings a curse.

The New Testament, as well as the Old Testament, clearly tells us God's word on staying sexually faithful to your marriage partner:

4 Let marriage be held in honor among all, and let the marriage bed be undefiled; for fornicators and adulterers God will judge.

—Hebrews 13

16 "For I hate divorce," says the Lord, the
God of Israel, "and him who covers his garment with wrong," says the Lord of hosts.
"So take heed to your spirit, that you do not
deal treacherously."

—Malachi 2

Remaining sexually pure is obviously extremely
important to God, and He expects a husband and
wife in the marriage relationship to remain sexually
pure and faithful. In fact, as we read earlier, the
Bible commands us to be happy with the wife of our
youth:

18 Let your fountain be blessed,
And rejoice in the wife of your youth.
19 As a loving hind and a graceful doe,
Let her breasts satisfy you at all times;
Be exhilarated always with her love.

—Proverbs 5

According to what we have read in this
chapter, the Bible does not condone adultery, which
has become so commonplace in the U.S. today.

To net it down, "no foolin' around." Be happy
with your wife and faithful to her. Like it or not,
it's in the Bible.

13

VIOLENCE
WITH SEXUAL OVERTONES

The scalping of white settlers by Indians did not start with the Indians. At one time, there was a reward for killing an Indian. The white men were the ones who started the scalping of the Indians, so that they could prove how many Indians they had killed. The Indians picked up this horrible practice from the white people.

Many years ago, I heard about a special, murderous force of the Chinese Army that was trained to kill women by cutting off their breasts and to kill men by cutting off their penises. This was even more repulsive to me than scalping. It made me want to vomit, because there seemed to be a sexual overtone to this gross violence.

King Saul was the very first king of Israel. After David killed Goliath, King Saul wanted him to come and be part of his court. Initially, David became endeared to King Saul. Later, however, Saul became afraid of him, for the Lord was with him. Saul offered David his daughter as a wife. This is what happened:

> 20 Now Michal, Saul's daughter, loved David. When they told Saul, the thing was agreeable to him.

21 And Saul thought, "I will give her to him that she may become a snare to him, and that the hand of the Philistines may be against him." Therefore Saul said to David, "For a second time you may be my son-in-law today."

22 Then Saul commanded his servants, "Speak to David secretly, saying, 'Behold, the king delights in you, and all his servants love you; now therefore, become the king's son-in-law.'"

23 So Saul's servants spoke these words to David. But David said, "Is it trivial in your sight to become the king's son-in-law, since I am a poor man and lightly esteemed?"

24 And the servants of Saul reported to him according to these words which David spoke.

25 Saul then said, "Thus you shall say to David, 'The king does not desire any dowry except a hundred foreskins of the Philistines, to take vengeance on the king's enemies.'" Now Saul planned to make David fall by the hand of the Philistines.

26 When his servants told David these words, it pleased David to become the king's son-in-law. Before the days had expired,

27 David rose up and went, he and his men, and struck down two hundred men among the Philistines. Then David brought their foreskins, and they gave them in full number to the king, that he might become the king's son-in-law. So Saul gave him Michal his daughter for a wife.

28 When Saul saw and knew that the Lord was with David, and that Michal, Saul's daughter, loved him,

29 then Saul was even more afraid of David. Thus Saul was David's enemy continually.

—1 Samuel 18

Can you imagine a more horrible dowry than portions of the penises of two hundred men? This was gross violence with definite sexual overtones. Yet with David, it gets worse.

Picture this scenario. Imagine that a king of some country—say Spain, Jordan or Saudi Arabi— lusted after a married lady and got her pregnant, while her husband was overseas in the army of the king. Then, in order to get rid of the husband, suppose the king sent orders to his general to get the husband and some other soldiers into a major battle and then to have the other soldiers withdraw, leaving the husband alone to fight. This would ensure that the husband would be killed, leaving his pregnant wife available for him to marry.

What would you think of such a king? Well, that is exactly what David did in the infamous story of David and Bathsheba. He saw a beautiful woman taking a bath next door, seduced her and made her pregnant, even though the woman was married.

> 2 Now when evening came David arose from his bed and walked around on the roof of the king's house, and from the roof he saw a woman bathing; and the woman was very beautiful in appearance.
> 3 So David sent and inquired about the woman. And one said, "Is this not Bathsheba, the daughter of Eliam, the wife of Uriah the Hittite?"
> 4 And David sent messengers and took her, and when she came to him, he lay with her; and when she had purified herself from her uncleanness, she returned to her house.
> 5 And the woman conceived; and she sent and told David, and said, "I am pregnant."
> —2 Samuel 11

David then decided to cover up his vile deed, by sending for her husband, who was on the war front, and getting him to come home and have sex with his wife, Bathsheba (the original Watergate). Then all would think that it was he who had gotten her pregnant rather than David:

> 6 Then David sent to Joab, saying, "Send me Uriah the Hittite." So Joab sent Uriah to David.
> 7 When Uriah came to him, David asked concerning the welfare of Joab and the people and the state of the war.
> 8 Then David said to Uriah, "Go down to your house, and wash your feet." And Uriah went out of the king's house, and a present from the king was sent out after him.
> 9 But Uriah slept at the door of the king's house with all the servants of his lord, and did not go down to his house.
> 10 Now when they told David, saying, "Uriah did not go down to his house," David said to Uriah, "Have you not come from a journey? Why did you not go down to your house?"
> 11 And Uriah said to David, "The ark and Israel and Judah are staying in temporary shelters, and my lord Joab and the servants of my lord are camping in the open field. Shall I then go to my house to eat and to drink and to lie with my wife? By your life and the life of your soul, I will not do this thing.
> 12 Then David said to Uriah, "Stay here today also, and tomorrow I will let you go." So Uriah remained in Jerusalem that day and the next.
> 13 Now David called him, and he ate and drank before him, and he made him drunk; and in the evening he went out to lie on his bed with his lord's servants, but he did not go down to his house.
>
> —2 Samuel 11

Uriah's loyalty to David was outstanding. He so wanted to serve David, that he did not even go home to his wife Bathsheba. Of course, this would not help David to cover up his sin, so then David essentially had him murdered. The story continues like this:

14 Now it came about in the morning that David wrote a letter to Joab, and sent it by the hand of Uriah.

15 And he had written in the letter, saying, "Place Uriah in the front line of the fiercest battle and withdraw from him, so that he may be struck down and die."

16 So it was as Joab kept watch on the city, that he put Uriah at the place where he knew there were valiant men.

17 And the men of the city went out and fought against Joab, and some of the people among David's servants fell; and Uriah the Hittite also died.

—2 Samuel 11

This is the most miserable chapter in David's life. God graciously allowed the illegitimate child to die that was born from David's abuse of Bathsheba. Later, when David and Bathsheba were legitimately married, she became the mother of Solomon.

16 David therefore inquired of God for the child; and David fasted and went and lay all night on the ground.

17 And the elders of his household stood beside him in order to raise him up from the ground, but he was unwilling and would not eat food with them.

18 Then it happened on the seventh day that the child died. And the servants of David were afraid to tell him that the child was

dead, for they said, "Behold, while the child was still alive, we spoke to him and he did not listen to our voice. How then can we tell him that the child is dead, since he might do himself harm!"

19 But when David saw that his servants were whispering together, David perceived that the child was dead; so David said to his servants, "Is the child dead?" And they said, "He is dead."

20 So David arose from the ground, washed, anointed himself, and changed his clothes; and he came into the house of the Lord and worshiped. Then he came to his own house, and when he requested, they set food before him and he ate.

21 Then his servants said to him, "What is this thing that you have done? While the child was alive, you fasted and wept; but when the child died, you arose and ate food."

22 And he said, "While the child was still alive, I fasted and wept; for I said, 'Who knows, the Lord may be gracious to me, that the child may live.'

23 "But now he has died; why should I fast? Can I bring him back again? I shall go to him, but he will not return to me."

24 Then David comforted his wife Bath-sheba, and went in to her and lay with her; and she gave birth to a son, and he named him Solomon. Now the Lord loved him.

—2 Samuel 12

From this story, we see that God can forgive anything, no matter how despicable it is, and give us a second chance. Today that forgiveness comes through the sacrificial death of God's Son, Jesus Christ.

14

VIOLENCE IN THE BIBLE

The Bible says that David was a man after God's own heart, yet David was a very warlike man who committed numerous acts of violence in his lifetime. God blessed him in the wars against his enemies, and essentially he always came out victorious.

There are times when David seemed to be extremely violent. In the story below, some men killed one of Saul's sons, thinking to do David a favor. In return, David not only killed them, but did something else, as you will see:

5 So the sons of Rimmon the Beerothite, Rechab and Baanah, departed and came to the house of Ish-bosheth in the heat of the day while he was taking his midday rest.

6 And they came to the middle of the house as if to get wheat, and they struck him in the belly; and Rechab and Baanah his brother escaped.

7 Now when they came into the house, as he was lying on his bed in his bedroom, they struck him and killed him and beheaded him. And they took his head and traveled by way of the Arabah all night.

8 Then they brought the head of Ish-bosheth to David at Hebron, and said to the king, "Behold, the head of Ish-bosheth, the son

of Saul, your enemy, who sought your life;
thus the Lord has given my lord the king
vengeance this day on Saul and his descen-
dants."

9 And David answered Rechab and Baanah
his brother, sons of Rimmon the Beerothite,
and said to them, "As the Lord lives, who has
redeemed my life from all distress,

10 when one told me, saying, 'Behold, Saul
is dead,' and thought he was bringing good
news, I seized him and killed him in Ziklag,
which was the reward I gave him for his news.

11 "How much more, when wicked men have
killed a righteous man in his own house on his
bed, shall I not now require his blood from
your hand, and destroy you from the earth?"

12 Then David commanded the young men,
and they killed them and cut off their hands
and feet, and hung them up beside the pool in
Hebron.   But they took the head of Ish-bosheth and buried it in the grave of Abner in
Hebron.

—2 Samuel 4

In verse 12, we see that David not only killed
these two men, but he cut off their hands and their
feet and hung them up beside the pool at Hebron.

On another occasion, David defeated the Philistines and then essentially played "Russian roulette"
with them. He killed two lines of the enemy and
left one alive to be his servants. He also hamstrung at least 1,000 horses.

1 Now after this it came about that David
defeated the Philistines and subdued them; and
David took control of the chief city from the
hand of the Philistines.

2 And he defeated Moab, and measured
them with the line, making them lie down on
the ground; and he measured two lines to put

to death and one full line to keep alive. And the Moabites became servants to David, bringing tribute.

3 Then David defeated Hadadezer, the son of Rehob king of Zobah, as he went to restore his rule at the River.

4 And David captured from him 1,700 horsemen and 20,000 foot soldiers; and David hamstrung the chariot horses, but reserved enough of them for 100 chariots.

5 And when the Arameans of Damascus came to help Hadadezer, king of Zobah, David killed 22,000 Arameans.

6 Then David put garrisons among the Arameans of Damascus, and the Arameans became servants to David, bring tribute. And the Lord helped David wherever he went.

—2 Samuel 8

Notice that verse 6 says that "the Lord helped David wherever he went."

ELIJAH KILLS PROPHETS OF BAAL

You may remember the story of the contest between Elijah and the 450 prophets of Baal. They each placed a sacrifice on a wooden altar and the prophets of Baal asked their god to send down fire to consume their sacrifice, which never occurred. Then, after drenching the sacrifice with water, Elijah asked God to send down fire from heaven and it not only consumed the sacrifice on the altar, but also the water in the trench! Let's read excerpts from that story:

22 Then Elijah said to the people, "I alone am left a prophet of the Lord, but Baal's prophets are 450 men.

23 "Now let them give us two oxen; and let them choose one ox for themselves and cut it

up, and place it on the wood, but put no fire under it; and I will prepare the other ox, and lay it on the wood, and I will not put a fire under it.

24 "Then you call on the name of your god, and I will call on the name of the Lord, and the God who answers by fire, He is God." And all the people answered and said, "That is a good idea."

25 So Elijah said to the prophets of Baal, "Choose one ox for yourselves and prepare it first for you are many, and call on the name of your god, but put no fire under it."

—1 Kings 18

This is an exciting story to read in its entirety. For the sake of space, let's read here just the end result of what happened:

37 "Answer me, O Lord, answer me, that this people may know that Thou, O Lord, art God, and that Thou hast turned their heart back again."

38 Then the fire of the Lord fell, and consumed the burnt offering and the wood and the stones and the dust, and licked up the water that was in the trench.

39 And when all the people saw it, they fell on their faces; and they said, "The Lord, He is God; the Lord, He is God."

40 Then Elijah said to them, "Seize the prophets of Baal; do not let one of them escape." So they seized them; and Elijah brought them down to the brook Kishon, and slew them there.

—1 Kings 18

As we read in the conclusion of this story, the people turned back to God. However, under God's command, Elijah took the 450 prophets of Baal and killed them, every one. This may seem a violent thing to do, but this was done under God's orders. It was an attempt to eradicate this false religion from the land and to get people to turn back to worshiping God Himself.

A MAN OF GOD ASSASSINATES THE KING

Some people might feel that the commandment, "Thou Shalt Not Kill" might apply to war or killing of false prophets, but that it certainly would never allow murder, and particularly murder of the king. However, there is a story in the Bible, that takes place when God first had the children of Israel captured, which indicates otherwise:

> 12 Now the sons of Israel again did evil in the sight of the Lord. So the Lord strengthened Eglon the king of Moab against Israel, because they had done evil in the sight of the Lord.
>
> 13 And he gathered to himself the sons of Ammon and Amalek; and he went and defeated Israel, and they possessed the city of the palm trees.
>
> 14 And the sons of Israel served Eglon the king of Moab eighteen years.
>
> —Judges 3

The reason that a foreign king and army came in and possessed their lands was that the children of Israel did evil in the sight of God. But the story does not end there. Finally, the children of Israel cried to the Lord, and the Lord raised up a deliverer for them—Ehud, a left-handed man of the tribe of Benjamin:

15 But when the sons of Israel cried to the Lord, the Lord raised up a deliverer for them, Ehud the son of Gera, the Benjamite, a left-handed man. And the sons of Israel sent tribute by him to Eglon the king of Moab.

16 And Ehud made himself a sword which had two edges, a cubit in length; and he bound it on his right thigh under his cloak.

17 And he presented the tribute to Eglon king of Moab. Now Eglon was a very fat man.

18 And it came about when he had finished presenting the tribute, that he sent away the people who had carried the tribute.

19 But he himself turned back from the idols which were at Gilgal, and said, "I have a secret message for you, O king." And he said, "Keep silence." And all who attended him left him.

20 And Ehud came to him while he was sitting alone in his cool roof chamber. And Ehud said, "I have a message from God for you." And he arose from his seat.

21 And Ehud stretched out his left hand, took the sword from his right thigh and thrust it into his belly.

22 The handle also went in after the blade, and the fat closed over the blade, for he did not draw the sword out of his belly; and the refuse came out.

23 Then Ehud went out into the vestibule and shut the doors of the roof chamber behind him, and locked them.

24 When he had gone out, his servants came and looked, and behold, the doors of the roof chamber were locked; and they said, "He is only relieving himself in the cool room."

25 And they waited until they became anxious; but behold, he did not open the doors of the roof chamber. Therefore they took the

key and opened them, and behold, their master had fallen to the floor dead.

—Judges 3

In this instance, we see that God raised up a deliverer who assassinated the head of the government. This is not just my perception of an action taken by a man of God; it is in the Bible.

WOMAN PRAISED AND BLESSED FOR MURDER

In the book of Judges, the children of Israel fell into the hands of Jabin, king of Cana. Jabin's commander in chief of his army was Sisera. God raised up Deborah, a prophetess, and told her:

> 7 'And I will draw out to you Sisera, the commander of Jabin's army, with his chariots and his many troops to the river Kishon; and I will give him into your hand.'"

—Judges 4

Then, later in that chapter we have a description of the war and what happened to Sisera, commander in chief of the Canaanite army:

> 13 And Sisera called together all his chariots, nine hundred iron chariots, and all the people who were with him, from Harosheth-hagoyim to the river Kishon.
> 14 And Deborah said to Barak, "Arise! For this is the day in which the Lord has given Sisera into your hands; behold, the Lord has gone out before you." So Barak went down from Mount Tabor with ten thousand men following him.
> 15 And the Lord routed Sisera and all his chariots and all his army, with the edge of the

sword before Barak; and Sisera alighted from his chariot and fled away on foot.

16 But Barak pursued the chariots and the army as far as Harosheth-hagoyim, and all the army of Sisera fell by the edge of the sword; not even one was left.

17 Now Sisera fled away on foot to the tent of Jael the wife of Heber the Kenite, for there was peace between Jabin the king of Hazor and the house of Heber the Kenite.

18 And Jael went out to meet Sisera, and said to him, "Turn aside, my master, turn aside to me! Do not be afraid." And he turned aside to her into the tent, and she covered him with a rug.

19 And he said to her, "Please give me a little water to drink, for I am thirsty." So she opened a bottle of milk and gave him a drink; then she covered him.

20 And he said to her, "Stand in the doorway of the tent, and it shall be if anyone comes and inquires of you, and says, 'Is there anyone here?' that you shall say, 'No.'"

21 But Jael, Heber's wife, took a tent peg and seized a hammer in her hand, and went secretly to him and drove the peg into his temple, and it went through into the ground; for he was sound asleep and exhaused. So he died.

22 And behold, as Barak pursued Sisera, Jael came out to meet him and said to him, "Come, and I will show you the man whom you are seeking." And he entered with her, and behold Sisera was lying dead with the tent peg in his temple.

—Judges 4

Here we have seen that Jael murdered the commander in chief of the other army. God's prophetess, Deborah, then blessed the woman who committed this murder:

> 1 Then Deborah and Barak the son of Abino sang on that day, saying, . . .
>
> 24 "Most blessed of women is Jael,
> The wife of Heber the Kenite;
> Most blessed is she of women in the tent.
> 25 "He asked for water and she gave him milk;
> 26 "She reached out her hand for the tent peg,
> And her right hand for the workmen's hammer.
> Then she struck Sisera, she smashed his head;
> And she shattered and pierced his temple.
> 27 "Between her feet he bowed, he fell, he lay;
> Between her feet he bowed, he fell;
> Where he bowed, there he fell dead.
> —Judges 5

Does it surprise you that a woman is praised for committing murder? Perhaps a God who would sanction such an action, through His prophetess of the day, does not fit into your image of the character of God, but it is in the Bible.

WAR, VIOLENCE AND MURDER

It is almost inconceivable for the average person to think of God as commanding war or commanding His people to do violent things, such as killing 450 prophets of another religion. The average person would not expect God to order someone to commit murder or to assassinate the ruler of the land. Yet the Bible clearly says that God did all of these things.

Let me hasten to add that this does not give us license to do violence or to murder. In the Scriptures, such acts could only be done legitimately when God commanded them. Today, we see an occasional wild man who commits violence of some kind claiming that God told him to do it. I cannot judge these people, but in my spirit I feel that, by and large, God had nothing to do with their acts.

However, we cannot rule out the possibility that sometime in the future God might clearly tell His people to do something specifically for Him that may involve violence and even the taking of life. In fact, the Bible clearly tells us that at least two Christians at some point in the future will do these sorts of things. These are the two witnesses found in the book of Revelation:

> 3 "And I will grant authority to my two witnesses, and they will prophesy for twelve hundred and sixty days, clothed in sackcloth."
> 4 These are the two olive trees and the two lampstands that stand before the Lord of the earth.
> 5 And if anyone desires to harm them, fire proceeds out of their mouth and devours their enemies; and if anyone would desire to harm them, in this manner he must be killed.
> —Revelation 11

This passage says that if anyone is going to harm these two witnesses, he *must* be killed by the fire that comes from their mouths.

Many Christians would be unwilling to devour their enemies (and God's enemies) with fire. Therefore, God certainly would not be able to utilize them in that capacity. I am not a redneck nor a violent man. It would cause me great grief, if God ever told me to kill someone. It would be totally contrary to my nature. However, I want to be willing to do anything that God commands me to do, including even an act of violence at His command. He has commanded His people to do acts of violence in times past, and there is no assurance that He will not do so once again way. God's character does not change.

Some people might feel that we do not have anything like this in the New Testament. Of course, the passage we just read from Revelation 11 is from the New Testament. Another verse they tend to overlook says that right at the end of Jesus' life, He commanded His followers to buy a sword, which today would be equivalent to telling His followers to buy a pistol or rifle:

> 35 And He said to them, "When I sent you out without purse and bag and sandals, you did not lack anything, did you?" And they said, "No, nothing."
> 36 And He said to them, "But now, let him who has a purse take it along, likewise also a bag, and let him who has no sword sell his robe and buy one. . . ."
>
> —Luke 22

While Jesus was here on the earth, His disciples went out without taking a purse or bag or sandals. However, right here at the end of His life, Jesus changed the ground rules. He told them to take a purse with them and, even if it meant selling one's robe, to buy and take a sword also (pistol or rifle), apparently for self-protection (not aggression). There would be no need to have a weapon, if they were not at least to be prepared to use it.

Again, what we have discussed in this chapter may stretch your image of God somewhat from what it has been. You may never have considered the fact that God has commanded certain acts of violence in times past and may again do so in the future. Believe it or not, *it's in the Bible.*

15

A GOD OF WAR?

As long as we are on the subject of violence, we might as well look at what the Bible has to say about war. This is an important topic, since terrorism, violence and the possibility of war seem to be ever increasing. What does the Bible have to say about war and violence, and what is God's opinion of war?

Many people believe that God is against war. Based on this, people have been "conscientious objectors," refusing to go into the military service because of their belief that God is against war.

In beginning to look at this subject, we need to realize that God does not change. He is the same yesterday, today and forever (Hebrews 13:8). Thus, what was true about God and war in the Old Testament is still true about Him today.

WOULD GOD COMMAND PEOPLE
TO GO TO WAR?

People have many different opinions about whether God would command people to go to war. Putting all of our opinions aside, let's look to see what the Bible has to say about this:

7 So they made war against Midian, just

"a mighty man of war" in Exodus 15:3 (KJV), which is included in the musical presentation, "The Messiah," by Handel.

Among the many possible examples that we could examine is the famous event at Jericho, when the walls fell down. Let's read about what God said to Joshua concerning Jericho:

> 1 Now Jericho was tightly shut because of the sons of Israel; no one went out and no one came in.
>
> 2 And the Lord said to Joshua, "See, I have given Jericho into your hand, with its king and the valiant warriors.
>
> 3 "And you shall march around the city, all the men of war circling the city once. You shall do so for six days. . . .
>
> 17 "And the city shall be under the ban, it and all that is in it belongs to the Lord; only Rahab the harlot and all who are with her in the house shall live, because she hid the messengers whom we sent. . . .
>
> 20 So the people shouted, and priests blew the trumpets; and it came about, when the people heard the sound of the trumpet, that the people shouted with a great shout and the wall fell down flat, so that the people went up into the city, every man straight ahead, and they took the city.
>
> 21 And they utterly destroyed everything in the city, both man and woman, young and old, and ox and sheep and donkey, with the edge of the sword. . . .
>
> 24 And they burned the city with fire, and all that was in it. Only the silver and gold and articles of bronze and iron, they put into the treasury of the house of the Lord.
>
> 25 However, Rahab the harlot and her father's household and all she had, Joshua

spared; and she has lived in the midst of
Israel to this day, for she hid the messengers
whom Joshua sent to spy out Jericho.

—Joshua 6

As you can see, the Lord commanded Joshua to
kill everyone in Jericho, except those in Rahab's
house. They were to kill the old people and the
young people, men and women. This would include
pregnant women who were about to deliver. (Not
only did they abort the baby; they also "aborted"
the mother!) They killed babies that were just one
day old, as well as old, feeble grandmothers.

There are, of course, numerous other specific
examples that we could take from the accounts of
the children of Israel conquering the promised land.
The Psalms tell us that it was God who was in
charge of that entire anniliation program:

1 O God, we have heard with our ears,
   Our fathers have told us,
   The work that Thou didst in their days,
   In the days of old.
2 Thou with Thine own hand didst drive
      out the nations;
   Then Thou didst plant them;
   Thou didst afflict the peoples,
   Then Thou didst spread them abroad.
3 For by their own sword they did not
      possess the land;
   And their own arm did not save them;
   But Thy right hand, and Thine arm, and
      the light of Thy presence,
   For Thou didst favor them.
4 Thou art my King, O God;
   Command victories for Jacob.
5 Through Thee we will push back our
      adversaries;
   Through Thy name we will trample
   down those who rise up against us.

6   For I will not trust in my bow,
    Nor will my sword save me.
7   But Thou hast saved us from our adver-
    saries,
    And thou has put to shame those who
    hate us.
8   In God we have boasted all day long,
    And we will give thanks to Thy name
    forever.

—Psalm 44

GOD TRAINS MEN FOR WAR

Even though God commanded war, it is hard
for us to think in terms of God training people for
war.   Yet we find in numerous places in the Old
Testament that tell us He did so:

1 Now these are the nations which the
Lord left, to test Israel by them (that is, all
who had not experienced any of the wars of
Canaan;
2 only in order that the generations of
the sons of Israel might be taught war, those
who had not experienced it formerly).

—Judges 3

34   He trains my hands for battle,
     So that my arms can bend a bow of
     bronze.
35   Thou hast also given me the shield of
     Thy salvation,
     And Thy right hand upholds me;
     And Thy gentleness makes me great.

—Psalm 18

In this passage in Psalms, we see that God
trained David's hands for battle.   Later in Psalms,
David came back to this same thought:

1 Blessed be the Lord, my rock,
   Who trains my hands for war,
   And my fingers for battle; . . .

—Psalm 144

CIVIL WAR

There are some wars that seem justifiable, wherein you are defending your country from outside invasion (such as when David defeated Goliath—1 Samuel 17). There are wars of conquest, such as God directing the children of Israel to conquer the promised land. All of these involve fighting with an outside enemy.

However, there are interesting situations in the Bible wherein some of the children of Israel fought with others who were also children of Israel, evidently at God's direction. The following is one such example. Some men from the tribe of Benjamin, who lived in Gibeah, had raped to death a man's concubine. The man cut his dead concubine into twelve pieces and sent the pieces to the tribes of Israel. The other tribes wanted the men responsible turned over, so they could put them to death. However, the men of the tribe of Benjamin refused and a civil war ensued. God evidently directed the other eleven tribes in this war:

11 Thus all the men of Israel were gathered against the city, united as one man.
12 Then the tribes of Israel sent men through the entire tribe of Benjamin, saying, "What is this wickedness that has taken place among you?
13 "Now then, deliver up the men, the worthless fellows in Gibeah, that we may put them to death and remove this wickedness from Israel." But the sons of Benjamin would not listen to the voice of their brothers, the sons of Israel.

14 And the sons of Benjamin gathered from
the cities to Gibeah, to go out to battle
against the sons of Israel. . . .

18 Now the sons of Israel arose, went up
to Bethel, and inquired of God, and said, "Who
shall go up first for us to battle against the
sons of Benjamin?"   Then the Lord said,
"Judah shall go up first." . . .

23 And the sons of Israel went up and wept
before the Lord until evening, and inquired of
the Lord, saying, "Shall we again draw near
for battle against the sons of my brother
Benjamin?" And the Lord said, "Go up against
him." . . .

27 And the sons of Israel inquired of the
Lord (for the ark of the covenant of God was
there in those days,

28 and Phinehas the son of Eleazar, Aaron's
son, stood before it to minister in those days),
saying, "Shall I yet again go out to battle
against the sons of my brother Benjamin, or
shall I cease?" And the Lord said, "Go up, for
tomorrow I will deliver them into your hand."

—Judges 20

GOD HIMSELF IS A WARRIOR,
A MAN OF WAR

We find many verses in the Bible which
portray God as a man of war. Here are some
examples:

13 The Lord will go forth like a warrior,
He will arouse His zeal like a man of
war.
He will utter a shout, yes, He will raise
a war cry.
He will prevail against His enemies.

—Isaiah 42

3   "The Lord is a warrior;
The Lord is His name. . . ."
—Exodus 15

14   "The Lord will fight for you while you
keep silent."
—Exodus 14

There has been much teaching on the armor of
God. However, most people who teach it, teach it
as though we are to create our own armor. That is
not the case. God's armor has existed from time
immemorial, and we are simply to put on *His* armor.
Let's read about this armor that God put on:

15   . . . Now the Lord saw,
And it was displeasing in His sight that
there was not justice.
16   And He saw that there was no man,
And was astonished that there was no
one to intercede;
Then His own arm brought salvation to
Him;
And His righteousness upheld Him.
17   And He put on righteousness like a
breastplate,
And a helmet of salvation on His head;
And He put on garments of vengeance
for clothing,
And wrapped Himself with zeal as a
mantle.
18   According to their deeds, so He will
repay,
Wrath to His adversaries, recompense to
His enemies;
To the coastlands He will make recom-
pense.
—Isaiah 59

The preceding passage describes God putting on His armor, dealing out wrath to His adversaries, and paying back His enemies. Verse 17 says that He puts on garments of vengeance for clothing.

When the nation of Israel was separated into two parts, Israel in the north and Judah in the south, we see God taking the side of the nation of Judah and killing 500,000 men:

> 13 But Jeroboam had set an ambush to come from the rear, so that Israel was in front of Judah, and the ambush was behind them.
> 14 When Judah turned around, behold, they were attacked both front and rear; so they cried to the Lord, and the priests blew the trumpets.
> 15 Then the men of Judah raised a war cry, and when the men of Judah raised the war cry, then it was that God routed Jeroboam and all Israel before Abijah and Judah.
> 16 And when the sons of Israel fled before Judah, God gave them into their hand.
> 17 And Abijah and his people defeated them with a great slaughter, so that 500,000 chosen men of Israel fell slain,
> 18 Thus the sons of Israel were subdued at that time, and the sons of Judah conquered because they trusted in the Lord, the God of their fathers.
>
> —2 Chronicles 13

There are numerous instances in the Bible in which God kills directly, by hail, plagues, swarms of insects or the earth swallowing people. Let's look at just two of them from the book of Numbers:

> 1 Now the people became like those who complain of adversity in the hearing of the Lord; and when the Lord heard it, His anger

was kindled, and the fire of the Lord burned among them and consumed some of the outskirts of the camp. . . .

33 While the meat was still between their teeth, before it was chewed, the anger of the Lord was kindled against the people, and the Lord struck the people with a very severe plague.

—Numbers 11

20 Then the Lord spoke to Moses and Aaron, saying,

21 "Separate yourselves from among this congregation, that I may consume them instantly."

22 But they fell on their faces, and said, "O God, Thou God of the spirits of all flesh, when one man sins, wilt Thou be angry with the entire congregation?"

23 Then the Lord spoke to Moses saying,

24 "Speak to the congregation, saying, 'Get back from around the dwellings of Korah, Dathan and Abiram.'"

25 Then Moses arose and went to Dathan and Abiram, with the elders of Israel following him,

26 and he spoke to the congregation, saying, "Depart now from the tents of these wicked men, and touch nothing that belongs to them, lest you be swept away in all their sin."

27 So they got back from around the dwellings of Korah, Dathan and Abiram; and Dathan and Abiram came out and stood at the doorway of their tents, along with their wives and their sons and their little ones.

28 And Moses said, "By this you shall know that the Lord has sent me to do all these deeds; for this is not my doing.

29 "If these men die the death of all men,

or if they suffer the fate of all men, then the Lord has not sent me.

30 "But if the Lord brings about an entirely new thing and the ground opens its mouth and swallows them up with all that is theirs, and they descend alive into Sheol, then you will understand that these men have spurned the Lord."

31 Then it came about as he finished speaking all these words, that the ground that was under them split open;

32 and the earth opened its mouth and swallowed them up, and their households, and all the men who belonged to Korah, with their possessions.

33 So they and all that belonged to them went down alive to Sheol; and the earth closed over them, and they perished from the midst of the assembly.

34 And all Israel who were around them fled at their outcry, for they said, "The earth may swallow us up!"

35 Fire also came forth from the Lord and consumed the two hundred and fifty men who were offering the incense.

—Numbers 16

There are other passages recorded, other than in the book of Numbers, in which God kills directly. We will take quite a few of these, but please read them all to acquaint yourself with this aspect of God's character:

7 But Er, Judah's first-born, was evil in the sight of the Lord, so the Lord took his life.

8 Then Judah said to Onan, "Go in to your brother's wife, and perform your duty as a brother-in-law to her, and raise up offspring for your brother."

9 And Onan knew that the offspring would not be his; so it came about that when he went in to his brother's wife, he wasted his seed on the ground, in order not to give offspring to his brother.

10 But what he did was displeasing in the sight of the Lord; so He took his life also.

—Genesis 38

2 "But the Lord said to me, 'Do not fear him, for I have delivered him and all his people and his land into your hand; and you shall do to him just as you did to Sihon king of the Amorites, who lived at Heshbon.' . . .

6 "And we utterly destroyed them, as we did to Sihon king of Heshbon, utterly destroying the men, women and children of every city. . . ."

22 'Do not fear them, for the Lord your God is the one fighting for you.' . . ."

—Deuteronomy 3

19 And He struck down some of the men of Bethemesh because they had looked into the ark of the Lord. He struck down of all the people, 50,070 men, and the people mourned because the Lord had struck the people with a great slaughter.

—1 Samuel 6

4 "And I shall make them an object of horror among all the kingdoms of the earth because of Manasseh, the son of Hezekiah, the king of Judah, for what he did in Jerusalem.

5 "Indeed, who will have pity on you, O
    Jerusalem,
    Or who will mourn for you,
    Or who will turn aside to ask about
    your welfare?

6 "You who have forsaken Me," declares
    the Lord,
"You keep going backward.
So I will stretch out My hand against
    you and destroy you;
I am tired of relenting!
7 "And I will winnow them with a winnow-
        ing fork
At the gates of the land;
I will bereave them of children, I will
        destroy My people;
They did not repent of their ways.
8 "Their widows will be more numerous
        before Me
Than the sand of the seas;
I will bring against them, against the
        mother of a young man,
A destroyer at noonday;
I will suddenly bring down on her
Anguish and dismay.
9 "She who bore seven sons pines away;
Her breathing is labored.
Her sun has set while it was yet day;
She has been shamed and humiliated.
So I shall give over their survivors to
        the sword
Before their enemies," declares the Lord.
                            —Jeremiah 15

11 And it came about as they fled from
before Israel, while they were at the descent
of Beth-horon, that the Lord threw large
stones from heaven on them as far as Azekah,
and they died; there were more who died
from the hailstones than those whom the sons
of Israel killed with the sword.
                            —Joshua 10

10 Now Samuel was offering up the burnt
offering, and the Philistines drew near to

battle against Israel. But the Lord thundered
with a great thunder on that day against the
Philistines and confused them, so that they
were routed before Israel.

—1 Samuel 7

20 And Jeroboam did not again recover
strength in the days of Abijah; and the Lord
struck him and he died.

—2 Chronicles 13

There were other times when God did not kill
directly, but He used His angels to kill people:

35 Then it happened that night that the
angel of the Lord went out, and struck 185,000
in the camp of the Assyrians; and when men
rose early in the morning, behold, all of them
were dead.

—2 Kings 19

From these and a whole host of other Scriptures, we see that God can, has and does kill
people, in certain instances.

31 The anger of God rose against them,
And killed some of their stoutest ones,
And subdued the choice men of Israel.
32 In spite of all this they still sinned,
And did not believe in His wonderful
works
33 So He brought their days to an end in
futility,
And their years in sudden terror.
34 When He killed them, then they sought
Him,
And returned and searched diligently for
God;
35 And they remembered that God was
their rock,

And the Most High God their Redeemer.

36 But they deceived Him with their
mouth,
And lied to Him with their tongue.

37 For their heart was not steadfast toward
Him,
Nor were they faithful in His covenant.

38 But He, being compassionate, forgave
their iniquities and did not destroy them;
And often He restrained His anger,
And did not arouse all His wrath.

39 Thus He remembered that they were but
flesh,
A wind that passes and does not return.

40 How often they rebelled against Him in
the wilderness,
And grieved Him in the desert!

41 And again and again they tempted God,
And pained the Holy One of Israel.

42 They did not remember His power,
The day when He redeemed them from
the adversary,

43 When He performed His signs in Egypt,
And His marvels in the field of Zoan,

44 And turned their rivers to blood,
And their streams, they could not
drink.

45 He sent among them swarms of flies,
which devoured them,
And frogs which destroyed them.

46 He gave also their crops to the grass-
hopper,
And the product of their labor to the
locust.

47 He destroyed their vines with hailstones,
And their sycamore trees with frost.

48 He gave over their cattle also to the
hailstones,

And their herds to bolts of lightning.
49 He sent upon them His burning anger,
Fury, and indignation, and trouble,
A band of destroying angels.
50 He leveled a path for His anger;
He did not spare their soul from death,
But gave over their life to the plague,
51 And smote all the first-born in
Egypt, . . .

—Psalm 78

PENALTY FOR DISOBEDIENCE

Most often God threatens to kill people if they do not obey Him and do not keep His commandments. There are a host of examples of this in the Old Testament. We will take just a couple of examples here:

12 And they entered into the covenant to seek the Lord God of their fathers with all their heart and soul;
13 and whoever would not seek the Lord God of Israel should be put to death, whether small or great, man or woman.
14 Moreover, they made an oath to the Lord with a loud voice, with shouting, with trumpets, and with horns.
15 And all Judah rejoiced concerning the oath, for they had sworn with their whole heart and had sought Him earnestly, and He let them find Him. So the Lord gave them rest on every side.

—2 Chronicles 15

5 "Indeed, who will have pity on you, O Jerusalem,
Or who will mourn for you,
Or who will turn aside to ask about your welfare?

6 "You who have forsaken Me," declares
the Lord,
"You keep going backward.
So I will stretch out My hand against
you and destroy you;
I am tired of relenting!
7 "And I will winnow them with a winnow-
ing fork
At the gates of the land;
I will bereave them of children, I will
destroy my people;
They did not repent of their ways. . . ."
—Jeremiah 15

Here in Jeremiah, we read that God is going
to destroy His people, because they forsook Him,
they did not repent, and they did not follow and
obey Him.

An even more drastic account says that if
people will not obey God, then horrible things will
happen:

21 'If then, you act with hostility against
Me are unwilling to obey Me, I will increase
the plague on you seven times according to
your sins.
22 'And I will let loose among you the
beasts of the field, which shall bereave you of
your children and destroy your cattle and
reduce your number so that your roads lie
deserted.
23 'And if by these things you are not
turned to Me, but act with hostility against
Me,
24 then I will act with hostility against
you; and I, even I will strike you seven times
for your sins.
25 'I will also bring upon you a sword
which will execute vengeance for the covenant;
and when you gather together into your cities,

I will send pestilence among you, so that you shall be delivered into enemy hands.

26 'When I break your staff of bread, ten women will bake your bread in one oven, and they will bring back your bread in rationed amounts, so that you will eat and not be satisfied.

27 'Yet if in spite of this, you do not obey Me, but act with hostility against Me,

28 then I will act with wrathful hostility against you; and I, even I, will punish you seven times for your sins.

29 'Further, you shall eat the flesh of your sons and the flesh of your daughters you shall eat.

30 'I then will destroy your high places, and cut down your incense altars, and heap your remains on the remains of your idols; for My soul shall abhor you.

31 'I will lay waste your cities as well, and will make your sanctuaries desolate; and I will not smell your soothing aromas.

32 'And I will make the land desolate so that your enemies who settle in it shall be appalled over it.

33 'You, however, I will scatter among the nations and will draw out a sword after you, as your land becomes desolate and your cities become waste. . . .'

—Leviticus 26

Here we see that for lack of obedience, the beasts will kill the children and fathers may even eat their sons. In the Old Testament, we see that God is a harsh God, a God of wrath and vengeance. In the New Testament, we see God as a God of compasssion, who sent His Son, Jesus Christ to die for us. Since God does not change, we know that He is not one or the other of these, but He is *both.* He still wants people to obey Him and serious consequences can result from disobedience. Yet, at the same time, He loves us very much, and He wants to do everything He can to help us come into a right relationship with Him through Jesus Christ.

If you are one who has assumed that the wrathful side of God's nature ended with the Old Testament, it might be helpful to read the following New Testament account of the return of Jesus Christ to the earth. Note that verse 11 says of Him that He "judges and wages war":

> 11 And I saw heaven opened; and behold, a white horse, and He who sat upon it is called Faithful and True; and in righteousness He judges and wages war.
>
> 12 And His eyes are a flame of fire, and upon His head are many diadems; and He has a name written upon Him which no one knows except Himself.
>
> 13 And He is clothed with a robe dipped in blood; and His name is called The Word of God.
>
> 14 And the armies which are in heaven, clothed in fine lineen, white and clean, were following Him on white horses.
>
> 15 And from His mouth comes a sharp sword, so that with it He may smite the nations; and He will rule them with a rod of iron; and He treads the wine press of the fierce wrath of God, the Almighty.
>
> 16 And on His robe and on His thigh He has a name written, "KING OF KINGS, AND LORD OF LORDS."
>
> —Revelation 19

JUST WARS AND CONSCIENTIOUS OBJECTORS

As we have just seen, when there was a call to war, God was very displeased with those who did not answer the call to arms. Thus, those in past wars who have claimed to be "conscientious objectors" cannot make the claim that the Bible is against war. Neither can they claim that God is against war or that God allows people to pick and choose which wars they will go to. It is also clearly in the Bible that we are to obey those who are set in authority over us:

> 1 Let every person be in subjection to the governing authorities. For there is no authority except from God, and those which exist are established by God.
> 2 Therefore he who resists authority has opposed the ordinance of God; and they who have opposed will receive condemnation upon themselves.
>
> —Romans 13

According to the Scriptures, even if the authorities running your country are fighting a war with which you disagree, you are still compelled to be patriotic and to go fight for your country and your government.

God is a God of righteousness and justice. Thus, He would never lead a nation into an unjust or an unrighteous war. Obviously the wise thing is for a nation to embark upon a war only when God directs it to and when it is a just and a righteous war.

TO HAVE GOD'S POWER AND HELP
WE MUST BE CLEAN

God expected the soldiers of the army to be pure and clean:

> 9 "When you go out as an army against your enemies, then you shall keep yourself from every evil thing.

10 "If there is among you any man who is unclean because of a nocturnal emission, then he must go outside the camp; he may not reenter the camp.

11 "But it shall be when evening approaches, he shall bathe himself with water, and at sundown he may reenter the camp.

12 "You shall also have a place outside the camp and go out there,

13 and you shall have a spade among your tools, and it shall be when you sit down outside, you shall dig with it and shall turn to cover up your excrement.

14 "Since the Lord your God walks in the midst of your camp to deliver you and to defeat your enemies before you, therefore your camp must be holy; and He must not see anything indecent among you lest He turn away from you. . . ."

—Deuteronomy 23

When God fights for you, you always win. No one is more powerful than He is.

3   There He broke the flaming arrows,
     The shield, and the sword, and the
         weapons of war.
4   Thou art resplendent,
     More majestic than the mountains of
         prey.
5   The stouthearted were plundered;
     They sank into sleep
     And none of the warriors could use his
         hands.
6   At Thy rebuke, O God of Jacob,
     Both rider and horse were cast into a
         dead sleep.
7   Thou, even Thou, art to be feared;
     And who may stand in Thy presence
         when once Thou art angry?

—Psalm 76

We could give a numerous examples from the Bible to show that God always wins. Sometimes, He would rain big hailstones on the enemy.   Other times, He would send great swarms of hornets or cause the enemy to see a huge but non-existent army.   One way or another, *if* God fights for you, you always win.   The key is to be certain that the army is clean and holy, so that God will fight for you.

16

DOES GOD BRING SICKNESS, EVIL AND DROUGHT ON PEOPLE?

We have just covered God commanding war, violence and murder. As if that were not enough, we are about to see that God has brought other very unpleasant things on people. I have heard some ministers say, "God would never make anyone sick." That is certainly not true, according to the Scriptures. God both allows people to become sick at times and, at other times, He directly causes sickness.

Obviously Satan can cause sickness—as in the case of Job—(Job 2:6-7) and he can send evil spirits on people (but only with God's permission). But God also has sent evil spirits on people, according to the Scriptures. He has brought drought to a land, sent plagues to a land and many other things of this nature. Let's look at some of these briefly, one at a time.

GOD BRINGS SICKNESS

There is no doubt about the fact that God clearly brings sickness to people. This is recorded repeatedly in the Scriptures:

28 But let a man examine himself, and so let him eat of the bread and drink of the cup.

29 For he who eats and drinks, eats and drinks judgment to himself, if he does not judge the body rightly.

30 For this reason many among you are weak and sick, and a number sleep.

31 But if we judged ourselves rightly, we should not be judged.

32 But when we are judged, we are disciplined by the Lord in order that we may not be condemned along with the world.

—1 Corinthians 11

Here we see clearly that in the New Testament times some were weak, some were sick and some had even died because they were treating the things of God in an incorrect manner. Things God did in the Old Testament, He still does today, just as as He did in Corinth during the days when the New Testament was written. Do not let anyone tell you that God has changed and will no longer make anyone sick. That is contrary to what the Scriptures say.

In addition to God bringing diseases, He also can be the one who causes more permanent ailments such as deafness, dumbness or blindness:

10 Then Moses said to the Lord, "Please, Lord, I have never been eloquent, neither recently nor in time past, nor since Thou has spoken to Thy servant; for I am slow of speech and slow of tongue."

11 And the Lord said to him, "Who has made man's mouth? Or who makes him dumb or deaf, or seeing or blind? Is it not I, the Lord? . . ."

—Exodus 4

20 "And behold, you shall be silent and unable to speak until the day when these things take place, because you did not believe my words, which shall be fulfilled in their proper time." ...

22 But when he came out, he was unable to speak to them; and they realized that he had seen a vision in the temple; and he kept making signs to them, and remained mute.

—Luke 1

3 And it came about that as he journeyed, he was approaching Damascus, and suddenly a light from heaven flashed around him;

4 and he fell to the ground, and heard a voice saying to him, "Saul, Saul, why are you persecuting Me?" ...

8 And Saul got up from the ground, and though his eyes were open, he could see nothing; and leading him by the hand, they brought him into Damascus.

9 And he was three days without sight, and neither ate nor drank. ...

17 And Ananias departed and entered the house, and after laying hands on him said, "Brother Saul, the Lord Jesus, who appeared to you on the road by which you were coming, has sent me so that you may regain your sight, and be filled with the Holy Spirit."

—Acts 9

GOD CAN ALSO HEAL

Just as surely as God can bring on sickness, God can also heal. In fact, approximately one-third of Christ's ministry, while He was here on the earth, was healing of the sick and the afflicted:

29 And departing from there, Jesus went along by the Sea of Galilee, and having gone up to the mountain, He was sitting there.

30 And great multitudes came to Him, bringing with them those who were lame, crippled, blind, dumb, and many others, and they laid them down at His feet; and He healed them,

31 so that the multitude marveled as they saw the dumb speaking, the crippled restored, and the lame walking, and the blind seeing; and they glorified the God of Israel.

—Matthew 15

56 And wherever He entered villages, or cities, or countryside, they were laying the sick in the market places, and entreating Him that they might just touch the fringe of His cloak; and as many as touched it were being cured.

—Mark 6

2 Now there is in Jerusalem by the sheep gate a pool, which is called in Hebrew Bethesda, having five porticoes.

3 In these lay a multitude of those who were sick, blind, lame, and withered, [waiting for the moving of the waters;

4 for an angel of the Lord went down at certain seasons into the pool, and stirred up the water; whoever then first, after the stirring up of the water, stepped in was made well from whatever disease with which he was afflicted.]

5 And a certain man was there, who had been thirty-eight years in his sickness.

6 When Jesus saw him lying there, and knew that he had already been a long time in that condition, He said to him, "Do you wish to get well?"

7 The sick man answered Him, "Sir, I have no man to put me into the pool when the water is stirred up, but while I am coming, another steps down before me."

8 Jesus said to him, "Arise, take up your pallet, and walk."

9 And immediately the man became well, and took up his pallet and began to walk.

—John 5

17 And Abraham prayed to God; and God healed Abimelech and his wife and his maids, so that they bore children.

—Genesis 20

Isn't it wonderful that God can heal, if we have faith, if we pray, and if we come to Him through Jesus Christ?

GOD BRINGS EVIL

God can also send evil spirits, whether they be deceiving spirits or lying spirits:

19 And Micaiah said, "Therefore, hear the word of the Lord. I saw the Lord sitting on His throne, and all the host of heaven standing by Him on His right and on His left.

20 "And the Lord said, 'Who will entice Ahab to go up and fall at Ramoth-gilead?' And one said this while another said that.

21 "Then a spirit came forward and stood before the Lord and said, 'I will entice him.'

22 "And the Lord said to him, 'How?' And he said, 'I will go out and be a deceiving spirit in the mouth of all his prophets.' Then He said, 'You are to entice him and also prevail. Go and do so.'

23 "Now therefore, behold, the Lord has put a deceiving spirit in the mouth of all these

your prophets; and the Lord has proclaimed
disaster against you."

—1 Kings 22

7 "Behold, I will put a spirit in him so
that he shall hear a rumor and return to his
own land.   And I will make him fall by the
sword in his own land.""

—2 Kings 19

God also sent an evil spirit upon King Saul.
We read about this in several places, two of which
are included here:

14 Now the Spirit of the Lord departed
from Saul, and an evil spirit from the Lord
terrorized him.
15 Saul's servants then said to him. "Behold now, an evil spirit from God is terror-
izing you. . . ."

—1 Samuel 16

10 Now it came about on the next day that
an evil spirit from God came mightily upon
Saul, and he raved in the midst of the house,
while David was playing the harp with his
hand, as usual; and a spear was in Saul's hand.
11 And Saul hurled the spear for he
thought, "I will pin David to the wall." But
David escaped from his presence twice.

—1 Samuel 18

23 Then God sent an evil spirit between
Abimelech and the men of Shechem; and the
men of Shechem dealt treacherously with
Abimelech, . . .

—Judges 9

It may seem strange to us that God would send evil spirits, but many people do not realize that God is the one who created the wicked and the evil:

> 4 The Lord has made everything for its own purpose,
> Even the wicked for the day of evil.
> —Proverbs 16

> 7 I form the light, and create darkness: I make peace, and create evil: I the Lord do all these things.
> —Isaiah 45, KJV

If God did not create evil, where did it come from? Did it create itself? As is seen in these verses, the Bible clearly teaches that God is the one who created evil. That may be contrary to your picture of God, but it is in the Bible. Since God is the one who made wickedness and evil, He certainly can control it.

GOD SENDS CALAMITIES

We tend to think of calamities as acts of nature or occurrences over which we have no control. We do not like to think of calamities as something that the Lord has brought, but the Bible clearly says that He can bring them:

> 6 If a trumpet is blown in a city will not the people tremble?
> If a calamity occurs in a city has not the Lord done it?
> —Amos 3

God can also send drought, and the famine that goes with it:

6   "But I gave you also cleanness of teeth
        in all your cities
And lack of bread in all your places,
Yet you have not returned to Me,"
    declares the Lord.
7   "And furthermore, I withheld the rain
        from you
While there were still three months un-
        til harvest.
Then I would send rain on one city
And on another city I would not send
        rain;
One part would be rained on,
While the other part not rained on
        would dry up.
8   "So two or three cities would stagger
        to another city to drink water,
But would not be satisfied;
Yet you have not returned to Me,"
    declares the Lord.
9   "I smote you with scorching wind and
        mildew;
And the caterpillar was devouring
Your many gardens and vineyards, fig
        trees and olive trees;
Yet you have not returned to Me,"
    declares the Lord.
10   "I sent a plague among you after the
        manner of Egypt;
I slew your young men by the sword
        along with your captured horses,
And I made the stench of your camp
        rise up in your nostrils;
Yet you have not returned to Me,"
    declares the Lord.
                                        —Amos 4

Many of you reading this book love the Lord,
as I do, and we all count on His lovingkindness and

compassion. However, in times past, the Lord has withdrawn His lovingkindness and compassion:

> 3 For thus says the Lord concerning the sons and daughters born in this place, and concerning their mothers who bear them, and their fathers who beget them in this land:
> 4 "They will die of deadly diseases, they will not be lamented or buried; they will be as dung on the surface of the ground and come to an end by sword and famine, and their carcasses will become food for the birds of the sky and for the beasts of the earth."
> 5 For thus says the Lord, "Do not enter a house of mourning, or go to lament or to console them, for I have withdrawn My peace from this people," declares the Lord, "My lovingkindness and compassion. . . ."
>
> —Jeremiah 16

If God has withdrawn His lovingkindness and compassion from His people in the Old Testament, He could certainly do so again, either from us as individuals or as a nation. This is a strong recommendation for America to turn back to God.

Prayer is a very important element in turning back to God, for an individual or a nation. Therefore, we need to take a good look at prayer, as there are some major misconceptions about it.

However, before we look at prayer, we need to remind ourselves that, just as God can take away, He can also restore.

We are all familiar with the story of Job, how he lost everything, including his wife, his children and all of his wealth. Ultimately, he even had boils all over his body. What many people lose sight of is the fact that the Lord can restore everything, as He did for Job!

10 And the Lord restored the fortunes of Job when he prayed for his friends, and the Lord increased all that Job had twofold.

11 Then all his brothers, and all his sisters, and all who had known him before, came to him, and they ate bread with him in his house; and they consoled him and comforted him for all the evil that the Lord had brought on him. And each one gave him one piece of money, and each a ring of gold.

12 And the Lord blessed the latter days of Job more than his beginning. . . .

—Job 42

The Lord gives and the Lord takes away. As we have seen in this chapter, sometimes the Lord sends sickness, evil spirits, plagues and calamities. However, it is wonderful to know that God also heals and He can restore and bless beyond what we can even ask or think (Ephesians 3:20; 1 Corinthians 2:9).

17

DON'T COUNT ON PRAYER

This may seem like a strange chapter title for a book concerning things that are in the Bible. We all have had the idea that when worse comes to worst, we can always turn to God in prayer. The popular opinion nowadays is that we are "all children of God," and there is a "brotherhood of mankind." The idea, whether it be true or false, is that we all have equal access to God.

The first thing we need to observe is that, according to the Scriptures, we are not all children of God. In talking to the Pharisees, Jesus had this to say:

> 44 "You are of your father the devil, and you want to do the desires of your father. He was a murderer from the beginning, and does not stand in the truth, because there is no truth in him. Whenever he speaks a lie, he speaks from his own nature; for he is a liar, and the father of lies. . . ."
>
> —John 8

Christ was telling the religious leaders that they were *not* children of God, but that they were children of the devil. Thus, Jesus Christ Himself divided everyone on the earth into two giant camps—those who are children of God (who have God as their father) and those who are children of the devil (who have the devil as their father). If you believe Jesus Christ, then you have to believe that we are not all children of God and, therefore, we do not all have the same access to God through prayer.

GOD DOES NOT ANSWER EVERYONE'S PRAYER

The concept that God does not answer everyone's prayer is found in both the Old and New Testaments. The prophet Isaiah said this:

> 1 Behold, the Lord's hand is not so short
> That it cannot save;
> Neither is His ear so dull
> That it cannot hear.
> 2 But your iniquities have made a sepa-
> ration between you and your God,
> And your sins have hidden His face
> from you, so that He does not hear.
> —Isaiah 59

This passage tells us that because of our iniquities (sin or disobeying God), God does not hear our prayers.

The same thought is repeated in the Psalms. For example:

> 18 If I regard wickedness in my heart,
> The Lord will not hear; . . .
> —Psalm 66

In this verse from the Psalms, we see that God does not hear us if we hold wickedness in our heart.   That wickedness may be unforgiveness, resentment, selfishness, hate, greed, sexual immorality or many other things.   If we hold those things in our heart, it says here clearly that God will not hear our prayers.

After King Saul began to pursue evil rather than God, the Bible tells us that he called on God, but God did not answer him:

> **37 And Saul inquired of God, "Shall I go down after the Philistines?   Wilt Thou give them into the hand of Israel?"   But He did not answer him on that day.**
>
> **—1 Samuel 14**

> **6 When Saul inquired of the Lord, the Lord did not answer him, either by dreams or by Urim or by prophets.**
>
> **—1 Samuel 28**

King Solomon is widely recognized as being the second wisest man ever to live (Jesus Christ, of course, being the wisest).   In Proverbs, Solomon tells us that the prayer (sacrifice) of the wicked is an abomination to the Lord:

> **8 The sacrifice of the wicked is an abomination to the Lord,**
> **But the prayer of the upright is His delight.**
>
> **—Proverbs 15**

> **29 The Lord is far from the wicked,**
> **But He hears the prayer of the righteous.**
>
> **—Proverbs 15**

We also learn that if an individual is upright, God delights in hearing his prayers.   Psalm 34 puts it this way:

15 The eyes of the Lord are toward the
righteous,
And His ears are open to their cry.
—Psalm 34

Through the prophet Isaiah, the Lord had this
message for the people of Sodom and Gomorrah
concerning prayer:

10 Hear the word of the Lord,
You rulers of Sodom;
Give ear to the instruction of our God,
You people of Gomorrah. . . .

15 "So when you spread out your hands in
prayer,
I will hide My eyes from you,
Yes, even though you multiply prayers,
I will not listen,
Your hands are covered with blood. . . ."
—Isaiah 1

The New Testament also clearly addresses this
subject of whether or not God hears all prayers.
It gives two significant criteria for God hearing our
prayers:

31 "We know that God does not hear sin-
ners; but if anyone is God-fearing, and does
His will, He hears him. . . ."
—John 9

We see here that a person must be first,
God-fearing and second, doing God's will, and then
God will hear him. Unfortunately, there are many
people, even Christians, who are not doing God's
will, yet they wonder why God does not answer
their prayers. Jesus Himself has told us why.

Now let us proceed to see what the Bible has
to say about how we *do* get our prayers answered.

18

HOW TO HAVE
YOUR PRAYERS ANSWERED

There are many Christians today who say that all we have to do is to ask for something from God, and we will automatically get it. They say that all we have to do is keep asking over and over, and God will eventually give us our request. Many people have the idea that they can pray for something, and then start claiming it, and it will happen. That concept does come from Scripture, but it is incomplete and cannot stand alone. Taken alone, I do not believe that it matches with what Jesus Christ taught and practiced about prayer. Such people are taking just a narrow segment of the Bible, because the Bible gives many other requirements to having our prayers answered, besides just asking. Let's examine them:

1. Pray in Jesus' Name

Praying Jesus' name means more than just tacking His name on the end of your prayer. It means coming to God with a heart attitude of submission, recognizing that you could not come to God at all except through the sacrifice of Jesus Christ on the cross. Also, if you have not received Him as your Savior, you do not have His name.

Thus, the following is for those who have Jesus Christ as their personal Savior:

> 23 "And in that day you will ask Me no question.   Truly, truly, I say to you, if you shall ask the Father for anything, He will give it to you in My name.
> 24 "Until now you have asked for nothing in My name; ask, and you will receive, that your joy may be made full. . . ."
>
> —John 16

2. We Must Pray Believing

Over and over again, faith is stated as a requirement for answered prayer:

> 21 And Jesus answered and said to them, "Truly I say to you, if you have faith, and do not doubt, you shall not only do what was done to the fig tree, but even if you say to this mountain, 'Be taken up and cast into the sea,' it shall happen.
> 22 "And all things you ask in prayer, believing, you shall receive."
>
> —Matthew 21

> 24 "Therefore I say to you, all things for which you pray and ask, believe that you have received them, and they shall be granted you. . . ."
>
> —Mark 11

Faith is not generated by positive confession or repeating over and over again that your prayer has already been answered.   Without a doubt, positive thinking has power, but it has nothing to do with faith and believing.   The Bible tells us where faith comes from:

> **17** So then faith cometh by hearing, and hearing by the word of God.
>
> —Romans 10, KJV

This says that faith comes by hearing "the word of God." However, if you take the time to check the Greek New Testament, this does not say that faith comes by hearing the *"logos"* of God —that is, faith does not come by hearing the Scriptures. The Greek word used here is *"rhema."* Correctly translated, faith comes by hearing the *"rhema"* of God.

The rhema of God is when the Holy Spirit speaks to your heart. The Holy Spirit can take a verse of Scripture and make it a rhema of God to you. However, you cannot randomly take a Scripture and start trying to make it the rhema of God for you, trying to have faith that God means that Scripture for you at that time.

Once the Holy Spirit speaks to your heart concerning something, you can know that it will happen. You may have had the same experience that I have had on many occasions, after seeking God about a particular request. In one instance, I had been praying for something for several weeks, then during a time of prayer God said, "it is yours." After that I could no longer ask God for it; I could only thank Him for it. I had received the rhema of God in that situation and it gave me total faith.

3. We Must Pray in God's Will

In order for our prayers to be answered, we have to pray in God's will. It may not be His will for us to be wealthy, for example. Jesus certainly was not wealthy, nor were His disciples. It may not always be God's will for someone to be healed. I believe this could be the case with Joni Eareckson Tada, a beautiful Christian woman who is a quadraplegic. She has had a wonderful ministry and has touched so very many lives for Christ in her glowing witness, since the accident that left her crippled. (Her spirit is not crippled!) Certainly Paul was not healed of his physical infirmity. We should all want whatever will bring *God* the most glory.

Prayer should begin with the Holy Spirit. If He lays it on your heart to pray for a certain thing, then it is the rhema of God to you, and you can know that it is the will of God.

> **14 And this is the confidence which we have before Him, that, if we ask anything according to His will, He hears us.**
> **15 And if we know that He hears us in whatever we ask, we know that we have the requests which we have asked from Him.**
> **—1 John 5**

If we are to pray in His will, prayer must begin with the Holy Spirit and not our own selfish desires.

4.   Pray Without Harboring Sin In Your Heart

As we saw in the last chapter, the Bible tells us that God will not hear sinners. I believe that includes Christians who are sinning (unless they are repenting). Here are two verses to refresh your memory:

> **31 "We know that God does not hear sinners; but if anyone is God-fearing, and does His will, He hears him. . . ."**
> **—John 9**

> **18 If I regard wickedness in my heart,**
>   **The Lord will not hear; . . .**
> **—Psalm 66**

If we are harboring and enjoying wickedness and known sin in our hearts, the Bible says that God will not even hear us, much less answer our prayers. Of course, He "hears us," in the sense that He hears every word spoken on the earth. What this means is that He does not receive our words as a prayer, if we are living in a way that is displeasing to Him. (There are exceptions to this, in that out of His mercy God may sometimes choose to answer our prayers in spite of our sin, but we have no guarantee that He will hear our prayers, if we are harboring sin in our lives.)

5. Pray Having Forgiven All

Many of us have old, old hurts, and we have never forgiven the people who have hurt us. This may have been a hurt inflicted by a parent or a close relative. It could have happened in our childhood or any other time in our past. If there is anyone that we have not forgiven, Jesus tells us that God will not forgive us. If He has not been able to forgive us because of our unforgiveness, then we still have iniquity in our heart. Here is what Jesus had to say on this:

14 "For if you forgive men for their transgressions, your heavenly Father will also forgive you.
15 "But if you do not forgive men, then your Father will not forgive your transgressions. . . ."

—Matthew 6

25 "And whenever you stand praying, forgive, if you have anything against anyone; so that your Father also who is in heaven may forgive you your transgressions.
26 ("But if you do not forgive, neither will

your Father who is in heaven forgive your transgressions.")

—Mark 11

You might want to pause and consider whether there is anyone in your past who has done you wrong, harmed you or hurt you, whom you have not forgiven. It does not matter whether or not that individual has repented or asked for forgiveness; God says you are to forgive him anyhow. If there is any unforgiveness in your heart, you might want to cry out to God right now and forgive that person. There is no need to live a moment longer with that unforgiveness blocking your forgiveness and clear communication with the Father.

6. Pray With Right Motives

If we pray with wrong motives, selfishly or for our own pleasure, the Bible says that God will not answer that prayer:

2 You lust and do not have; so you commit murder. And you are envious and cannot obtain; so you fight and quarrel. You do not have because you do not ask.

3 You ask and do not receive, because you ask with wrong motives, so that you may spend it on your pleasures.

—James 4

7. Pray Not As A Friend Of The World

The world has a lot to offer, but if we are friends of the world, we make ourselves enemies of God. I do not believe that God will answer the prayers of His enemies:

HOW TO HAVE YOUR PRAYERS ANSWERED   185

15 Do not love the world, nor the things in the world. If anyone loves the world, the love of the Father is not in him.

16 For all that is in the world, the lust of the flesh and the lust of the eyes and the boastful pride of life, is not from the Father, but is from the world.

—1 John 2

4 You adulteresses, do you not know that friendship with the world is hostility toward God? Therefore whoever wishes to be a friend of the world makes himself an enemy of God.

—James 4

8.   Keep On Praying

When Christ said to "ask and you will receive," the Greek actually says "*keep on asking* and you will receive." Williams, who translated a version of the New Testament (which was initially published by Moody Press but is now published by Broadman Press), pointed out that the verbs in connection with prayer are in the continuous tense. For example, Matthew 8:7,8 is best translated:

7 Keep on asking, and it will be given to you; Keep on seeking, and you will find; keep on knocking (reverently) and the door will be opened to you.

8 For every one who keeps on asking receives, and he who keeps on seeking finds, and to him who keeps on knocking it will be opened.

—Matthew 7, Amplified

All of the teaching of Christ on prayer portrayed this "continuous asking" form of prayer. *The Amplified Bible* again reflects this well in the following passage:

1 Then He was praying in a certain place, and when He stopped, one of His disciples said to Him, Lord, teach us to pray, as John taught his disciples.

2 And He said to them, When you pray, say, (Our) Father, (Who is in heaven,) hallowed be Your name. Your kingdom come. Your will be done—held holy and revered—on earth as it is in heaven.

3 Give us daily our bread (food for the morrow),

4 And forgive us our sins, for we ourselves also forgive every one who is indebted to us—who has offended us or done us wrong; and bring us not into temptation, but rescue us from evil.

5 And He said to them, Which of you who has a friend will go to him at midnight and will say to him, Friend, lend me three loaves (of bread),

6 For a friend of mine who is on a journey has just come, and I have nothing to put before him;

7 And he from within will answer, Do not disturb me; the door is now closed, and my children are with me in bed; I cannot get up and supply you (with anything)?

8 I tell you, although he will not get up and supply him anything because he is his friend, yet because of his shameless persistence and insistence, he will get up and give him as much as he needs.

9 So I say to you, Ask and keep on asking, and it shall be given you; seek and keep on seeking, and you shall find; knock and keep on knocking and the door shall be opened to you.

10 For every one who asks and keeps on asking receives, and he who seeks and keeps

on seeking finds, and to him who knocks and
keeps on knocking the door shall be opened.
—Luke 11, Amplified

The *New American Standard Bible* gives the
continuous tense in the marginal notes for the last
two verses: *"keep asking, keep seeking, keep
knocking."* This fits in perfectly with the example
that Christ just gave—that of going to a friend at
midnight and persistently asking. The main thing to
note here is that the Greek tells us not to ask just
once and then start "claiming" or "confessing" it.
The Bible actually tells us to keep on asking.

Another example of prayer that Christ gave
along this same line involved a woman going to a
judge:

1 Now He was telling them a parable to
show that at all times they ought to pray and
not to lose heart,

2 saying, "There was in a certain city a
judge who did not fear God, and did not
respect man.

3 "And there was a widow in that city,
and she kept coming to him, saying, 'Give me
legal protection from my opponent.'

4 "And for a while he was unwilling; but
afterward he said to himself, 'Even though I
do not fear God nor respect man,

5 yet because this widow bothers me, I
will give her legal protection, lest by
continually coming she wear me out.'"

6 And the Lord said, "Hear what the unrighteous judge said;

7 now shall not God bring about justice
for His elect, who cry to Him day and night,
and will He delay long over them? . . ."
—Luke 18

Jesus wanted His disciples to keep on praying and not to lose heart, so He told them about this woman who kept coming to the judge day after day. Thus, we see that, according to the teachings of Jesus, we do not just pray once and then start claiming that we have the answer. We "keep on praying" day after day. We should pray continually. *The Amplified Bible* gives an even better feeling for verse 1:

1 Also [Jesus] told them a parable, to the effect that they ought always to pray and not to turn coward—faint, lose heart and give up.
—Luke 18, Amplified

This persistence in prayer is found many places in the Scriptures:

17 Pray without ceasing; . . .
—1 Thessalonians 5

18 With all prayer and petition pray at all times in the Spirit, and with this in view, be on the alert with all perseverance and petition for all the saints, . . .
—Ephesians 5

Jesus prayed multiple times for things:

44 And He left them again, and went away and prayed a third time, saying the same thing once more.
—Matthew 26

9. Obey God and Please Him

Another requirement for having our prayers answered is that we obey God's commandments and do the things that are pleasing to Him:

22 and whatever we ask we receive from Him, because we keep His commandments and do the things that are pleasing in His sight.
—1 John 3

You could think of this another way. In order to have our prayers answered, we need to avoid doing things that displease God.

JESUS PRAYED FOR LONG PERIODS OF TIME

We know that Christ frequently got up a great while before dawn to pray and, on one occasion of which we are aware, He prayed all night long:

35 And in the early morning, while it was still dark, He arose and went out and departed to a lonely place, and was praying there.
—Mark 1

12 And it was at this time that He went off to the mountain to pray, and He spent the whole night in prayer to God.
—Luke 6

SUMMARY AND CONCLUSION

Shortly after I became a Christian and God began showing me these things, I was preaching at a small church on the outskirts of Dallas. I talked about prayer and that God did not answer the prayers of an unbeliever. At the end of this service, a man came forward and received Jesus Christ as his personal Savior. Then he gathered his two little girls, one in each arm, and with tears running down his cheeks, he said, "Now Daddy can pray for you and God will hear his prayers." This man came to realize that if his daughters got sick, even if he prayed for them to get well, God was not under any obligation to hear or to answer his prayer. But now, with his new relationship with God the Father through Jesus Christ, he could indeed pray for his girls, and God would hear and answer.

Many people falsely assume that when they pray for a business deal to turn out right, or they pray for a loved one to get well, God will hear their prayers. As we have seen from the Scriptures, this is not necessarily true, unless they are living in a right relationship with God, doing His will and living an upright life. God wants everyone to come into a right relationship with Him, so that He can hear and answer their prayers.

It is much like a parent who has a child who is rebellious and has run off or is involved with dope, violence or other evil things. That parent may indeed wish to give that son or daughter a sum of money or a portion of his business. However, he cannot afford to do that, until that son or daughter returns, cleans up his or her life and becomes rightly related to the parents once again, without any rebellion in his heart. God is the same way. He wants those in rebellion against Him to come into a right relationship with Him, so that He can give them the wonderful blessings and the happy life that He desires for them.

God wants to have clear communication with all of us, not blocked by any of the hindrances we have discussed in this chapter.

19

WINE AND STRONG DRINK

When you bring up subjects of behavior, such as the drinking of wine, Christians tend to have very strong emotions concerning these subjects, either for or against. I would like to share an event which indicates that, to a great extent, these strong reactions are cultural in origin. This event happened right after World War II.

InterVarsity Christian Fellowship held a world convention in Europe. At that time, no Christian woman in Europe, no matter how liberal, wore lipstick. All the American girls came in wearing lipstick and the Christian girls of Europe ran up to Stacy Woods, then President of IVCF International, and asked if these American girls were Christians, because they were wearing lipstick. He pointed out to them that in America it was okay for a Christian to wear lipstick.

Of course, wine was served with the meal, because all Christians in Europe drank wine with their meals. This shocked the American delegation. So, immediately after the meal, the American girls rushed up to Stacy Woods to ask him if these European girls were Christians, because they drank wine with the meal. He explained to them that in their culture, this was perfectly acceptable.

The problem with most of us is that much of what we have learned about Christianity is based on culture and not on the Bible. It is difficult for many of us to examine, with an open mind, what the Bible actually has to say about subjects that many people's upbringing condemns so strongly. Please, breathe a little prayer that God will help you to examine with an open heart and mind what the Bible does say about this subject of drinking wine.

DRINKING WINE
IS COMMENDED AND COMMANDED

It may surprise many Christians that drinking wine is actually advocated in the Bible:

> 7 Go then, eat your bread in happiness, and drink your wine with a cheerful heart; for God has already approved your works.
> 8 Let your clothes be white all the time, and let not oil be lacking on your head.
> 9 Enjoy life with the woman whom you love all the days of your fleeting life which He has given to you under the sun; for this is your reward in life, and in your toil in which you have labored under the sun.
> —Ecclesiastes 9

Verse 7 tells the people to drink wine with a cheerful heart. This is not a command, but it is something that the people are certainly allowed to enjoy, with God's sanction. The Bible goes further; the book of 1 Timothy actually instructs that wine be used:

> 23 No longer drink water exclusively, but use a little wine for the sake of your stomach and your frequent ailments.
> —1 Timothy 5

In addressing the coming thousand-year reign of Jesus Christ here on the earth, when all the hills will have been dissolved, the Bible says that during this period (the millennium) God's people will be drinking wine:

13   "Behold, days are coming," declares the
         Lord,
      "When the plowman will overtake the
         reaper
      And the treader of grapes him who
         sows seed;
      When the mountains will drip sweet
         wine,
      And all the hills will be dissolved.
14   "Also I will restore the captivity of My
         people Israel,
      And they will rebuild the ruined cities
         and live in them,
      They will also plant vineyards and
         drink their wine,
      And make gardens and eat their fruit.
15   "I   will also plant them on their land,
      And they will not again be rooted out
         from their land
      Which I have given them,"
      Says the Lord your God.
                                    —Amos 9

In the days of the New Testament, most of the water was contaminated and many people only drank wine. Without refrigeration, grape juice could not be kept without it turning into vinegar, unless they converted it into wine.

THAT WINEMAKER

Jesus Christ certainly would not make anything that was intrinsically bad. Yet, there is solid bibli-

cal evidence that He made wine at a wedding feast.
In fact, this was His first miracle:

> 1 And on the third day there was a
> wedding in Cana of Galilee, and the mother of
> Jesus was there;
> 2 and Jesus also was invited, and His dis-
> ciples, to the wedding.
> 3 And when the wine gave out, the mother
> of Jesus said to Him, "They have no wine."
> 4 And Jesus said to her, "Woman, what do
> I have to do with you? My hour has not yet
> come."
> 5 His mother said to the servants, "What-
> ever He says to you, do it."
> 6 Now there were six stone waterpots set
> there for the Jewish custom of purification,
> containing twenty or thirty gallons each.
> 7 Jesus said to them, "Fill the waterpots
> with water." And they filled them up to the
> brim.
> 8 And He said to them, "Draw some out
> now, and take it to the headwaiter." And
> they took it to him.
> 9 And when the headwaiter tasted the wa-
> ter which had become wine, and did not know
> where it came from (but the servants who had
> drawn the water knew), the headwaiter called
> the bridegroom,
> 10 and said to him, "Every man serves the
> good wine first, and when men have drunk
> freely, then that which is poorer; you have
> kept the good wine until now."
> 11 This beginning of His signs Jesus did in
> Cana of Galilee, and manifested His glory, and
> His disciples believed in Him.
> —John 2

The headwaiter commented to the bridegroom
that people usually started with the good wine and

then, after people were somewhat drunk, they brought out the poorer-quality wine. Yet the headwaiter said that the wine which Jesus made was the best that had been served. Certainly the headwaiter knew good wine from bad.

There are some people who would say that Jesus did not create wine, but created a "heavenly nectar." However, exactly the same Greek word (*oinos*) is used here as is used when the good Samaritan poured *wine* into the wounds of the stranger who had been beaten up and left lying by the wayside. The good Samaritan certainly would not have poured grape juice into wounds, which would only have attracted flies; he would have used wine with an alcoholic content.

Thus, we see Jesus Himself making wine. Not only that, but He evidently drank wine on a regular basis:

> 33 For John the Baptist came neither eating bread nor drinking wine; and ye say, He hath a devil.
> 34 The Son of man is come eating and drinking; and ye say, Behold a gluttonous man, and a winebibber, a friend of publicans and sinners!
>
> —Luke 7, KJV

> 19 "The Son of Man came eating and drinking, and they say, 'Behold, a gluttonous man and a drunkard, a friend of tax-gatherers and sinners!' Yet wisdom is vindicated by her deeds."
>
> —Matthew 11

Apparently, it was common knowledge that Jesus drank wine (*oinos*). Yet, we know that Jesus was without sin (Hebrews 4:15). So, evidently drinking wine (in moderation) is not a sin.

At one time, I was leading a Bible study in Poughkeepsie, New York. There were a number of Ph.D.'s and people with master's degrees attending. Intellectually, it was quite a high-level Bible study. When we discussed the subject of drinking wine, one lady—who had a master's degree in physics— said this: "But wouldn't a Christian who did not drink wine be just a little bit better than another Christian who did drink wine?" My reply was that if she wanted to consider herself just a little bit better than Jesus, she was welcome to adopt that attitude, but it might not be very wise.

INTOXICATION FORBIDDEN

Even though the Bible gives liberty to drink wine, the Bible has strong words about becoming intoxicated; that is really forbidden:

18 And do not get drunk with wine, for that is dissipation, but be filled with the Holy Spirit, . . .

—Ephesians 5

1 Wine is a mocker, strong drink a brawler, And whoever is intoxicated by it is not wise.

—Proverbs 20

God wants to be in control of an individual. When wine or strong drink gains control, as it does with intoxication, then God is edged out and is no longer in control of that individual. In reading about requirements for our church leaders, as found in Timothy, we find that they must not be addicted to wine:

1 It is a trustworthy statement: if any man aspires to the office of overseer, it is a fine work he desires to do.

2 An overseer, then, must be above reproach, the husband of one wife, temperate, prudent, respectable, hospitable, able to teach,

3 not addicted to wine or pugnacious, but gentle, uncontentious, free from the love of money.

—1 Timothy 3

A person addicted to wine is really to be pitied. The wise King Solomon had this to say about it:

29 Who has woe? Who has sorrow?
    Who has contentions? Who has
        complaining?
    Who has wounds without cause?
    Who has redness of eyes?
30 Those who linger long over wine,
    Those who go to taste mixed wine.
31 Do not look on the wine when it is red,
    When it sparkles in the cup,
    When it goes down smoothly;
32 At the last it bites like a serpent,
    And stings like a viper.
33 Your eyes will see strange things,
    And your mind will utter perverse
        things.
34 And you will be like one who lies down
        in the middle of the sea,
    Or like one who lies down on the top
        of a mast.
35 "They struck me, but I did not become
        ill;
    They beat me, but I did not know it.
    When shall I awake?
    I will seek another drink."

—Proverbs 23

EACH MAN MUST FOLLOW GOD

During the early years of this century, there was a form of "holiness" popularized in some Christian circles that I believe was artificial. Women could not wear makeup, and so forth. God may have led some individuals in this way, but they then tried to make what God was telling them a universal rule for all people. There is a new call of holiness going out to Christians today, but in it each individual is going to have to follow the leading of God. What may be sin for one person, may not be for another.

For example, I knew a man who was addicted to baseball. He became a Christian and God told him that he could not go to baseball games. When he found out that other Christian men went to baseball games, he was absolutely shocked. God wanted to be the center of His life, instead of baseball. As is often the case, whatever has been in the center, God will remove, whether on a temporary or permanent basis. This has been true for many Christians.

The principle of each individual following God can result in a situation wherein one Christian feels it is okay to drink wine and another feels that it is absolutely sinful. A similar controversy was raging during the first century. People would take animals and sacrifice them at pagan temples. There was far more meat there than the priests could eat, so they sold the excess at a cut rate out the back door. Some Christians felt it was just fine to eat this meat, while others felt that it was a terrible sin:

4 Therefore concerning the eating of things sacrificed to idols, we know that there is no such thing as an idol in the world, and that there is no God but one. . . .

7 However not all men have this knowledge; but some, being accustomed to the idol

until now, eat food as if it were sacrificed to
an idol; and their conscience being weak is
defiled.

8 But food will not commend us to God;
we are neither the worse if we do not eat,
nor the better if we do eat.

9 But take care lest this liberty of yours
somehow become a stumbling block to the weak.

—1 Corinthians 8

1 Now accept the one who is weak in
faith, but not for the purpose of passing
judgment on his opinions.

2 One man has faith that he may eat all
things, but he who is weak eats vegetables
only.

3 Let not him who eats regard with
contempt him who does not eat, and let not
him who does not eat judge him who eats, for
God has accepted him.

—Romans 14

The last verse of Romans 14 is really the key.
We are each servants of God, and who are we to
judge another's servant?   That individual is going
to stand or fall before God, depending on whether
he is obeying God or following the lust of his own
flesh.

It is also interesting to note that the weaker
brother is described as the one who does the
abstaining, whereas the person more mature in the
faith has the liberty to eat all things.   I believe
the reason for this is that a mature person is
listening to God on a moment-by-moment basis.   He
will abstain whenever God tells him to do so, and
he will only partake when God gives him the
liberty.

Paul concludes the chapter in Romans on this
controversy in a very significant way:

religion and self-abasement and severe treat-
ment of the body, but are of no value against
fleshly indulgence.

—Colossians 2

In the preceding passage, we see that little
rules like, "Do not taste this" and "Do not touch
that" appear to have a righteousness to them, but
the last verse tells us that they are of "no value"
against fleshly indulgence.   It is not little rules
that make one live a righteous, holy and pure life.
It is a personal relationship with God, through
Jesus Christ, and a devout love for Him.

In this chapter, we have seen that the Bible
does not condemn the drinking of wine, as some
people do.   This may come as a surprise to some,
who perhaps have assumed that the Bible did
condemn wine drinking.   We have seen that Jesus
made and drank wine and that the Bible instructs us
to drink wine "with a cheerful heart," or to use a
little wine for certain ailments.

However, becoming intoxicated is decidedly
forbidden, as is allowing our liberty to become a
stumbling block for a weaker brother.   The bottom
line is that, in this matter, as in any other, we
need to seek the Lord's guidance on each occasion
as to whether or not we should drink wine, and
then drink or abstain according to how He directs
us.

God may not want you ever to drink wine or
strong drink, as was the case with Samson.   The
angel of the Lord told Samson's mother that he was
to be a Nazarite.   Part of the Nazarite vow was to
abstain from wine and strong drink:

3 Then the angel of the Lord appeared to
the woman, and said to her, "Behold now, you
are barren and have borne no children, but
you shall concieve and give birth to a son.

4 "Now, therefore, be careful not to drink wine or strong drink, nor eat any unclean thing.

5 "For behold, you shall concieve and give birth to a son, and no razor shall come upon his head, for the boy shall be a Nazarite to God from the womb; and he shall begin to deliver Israel from the hands of the Philistines."

—Judges 13

2 "speak to the sons of Israel, and say to them, 'When a man or woman makes a special vow, the vow of a Nazarite, to dedicate himself to the Lord,

3 he shall abstain from wine and strong drink; he shall drink no vinegar, whether made from wine or strong drink, neither shall he drink any grape juice, nor eat fresh or dried grapes. . . .'"

—Numbers 6

Although Samson's mother and Samson and others have been directed to abstain from wine and strong drink, it does not follow that one can impose a characteristic onto God that He disapproves of drinking wine. To do so is not in keeping with the rest of what the Bible has to say on this subject.

BE CAREFUL NOT TO "ADD TO GOD"

There are numerous admonitions that we should not add anything to the Scriptures:

18 I testify to everyone who hears the words of the prophecy of this book: if anyone adds to them, God shall add to him the plagues which are written in this book; . . .

—Revelation 22

6 Do not add to His words
Lest He reprove you, and you be proved
a liar.
—Proverbs 30

Paul also tells us not to go beyond that which is written:

6 Now these things, brethren, I have figuratively applied to myself and Apollos for your sakes, that in us you might learn not to exceed what is written, in order that no one of you might become arrogant in behalf of one against the other.
—1 Corinthians 4

I am here to tell you that it is even worse to add something to God than it is to add something to God's word. If you try to add a characteristic to God that He does not have—that He is against drinking wine, for instance—then you are attributing to Him an attitude that He does not have, and that is very dangerous.

Almost all of the Christians in Europe drink wine freely. When I was a young man growing up, I heard about the "beer-drinking Lutherans." There are a host of people on this planet who are born again and love Jesus Christ with all their hearts, who believe it is all right for them to drink wine. For you to condemn them because you believe God is against it is treading on very dangerous ground, since you have no biblical basis for doing so.

There are some who would say that the wine in the Bible was really vinegar. This is a distortion of Scriptures, since the Bible talks about drinking wine in order to make the heart merry. Also, can you see Jesus coming into a Pharisee's house and drinking a glass of vinegar?

There are others who say that the Bible is against drugs (sorcery, "*pharmakeia*" in the Greek —medication by witchcraft), and there is truth to this assertion. However, there is absolutely no way that one can twist the meaning of these words and make wine fit the category of sorcery. Wine was an everyday beverage.

There are numerous ministers I know personally, who drink wine in their own homes or in a very dark corner of a restaurant, who would never drink it publicly where anyone could see them. I don't believe that hiding this practice and putting up a false front will help the sheep. Pastors, I would encourage you to be honest with your flock.

When I was pastor of Catalina Bible Church on Catalina Island, I told the congregation at the very beginning that I believed that it was legitimate, according to the Scriptures, to drink wine. I also told them that I knew that some of them did not believe in this, so I would absolutely abstain from anything alcoholic as long as I was pastor (it was not that important to me). However, I told them that when I came to that subject in the Bible, I was going to preach it like I believed it. A couple of years later, one of the elders said to me that he had felt that most people who believed it was okay to drink wine did so just as an excuse for an indulgence. He then told me that I had convinced him, since I was not using my belief as an excuse for indulgence; I was simply preaching truth from the Scriptures as I saw it.

In examining my heart, as far as I am aware, there is nothing included in this book that is written for my own self indulgence. What I yearn to do is to help you break off all of those artificial limbs that people have tried to graft onto God, which are not part of who He is. It is my desire to help you see Him clearly as He is and worship, adore and obey the wonderful God of the Bible.

20

USE OF THE TITHE

Most people know that a tithe is 10 percent. Sometimes the Bible refers to this as 10 percent of your income, and other times it is 10 percent of your increase. However, for most people these are synonomous, so we will simply look at it as 10 percent of the income. The Bible is very strict in its assertion that the tithe belongs to God:

8 "Will a man rob God? Yet you are robbing Me! But you say, 'How have we robbed Thee?' In tithes and offerings.
9 "You are cursed with a curse, for you are robbing Me, the whole nation of you! . . ."
—Malachi 3

According to this passage, if a believer is not tithing, he is robbing God and he is under a curse. Jesus reiterated the tithe when He told the Pharisees the following:

23 "Woe to you, scribes and Pharisees, hypocrites! For you tithe mint and dill and cummin, and have neglected the weightier provisions of the law: justice and mercy and faithfulness; but these are the things you

should   have   done   without   neglecting   the
others. . . ."

—Matthew 23

42 "But woe to you Pharisees!   For you pay
tithe of mint and rue and every kind of garden herb, and yet disregard justice and the
love of God; but these are the things you
should have done without neglecting the
others. . . ."

—Luke 11

Here Jesus told the Pharisees that they should
tithe, but they should not neglect the more
important things of the law.

What we need to realize very clearly is that
the tithe belongs to God—*period.*

There have been cases in which a poor person
came to the back door of a Christian's home and
asked for a little money for food, and the Christian
said, "I cannot give you anything, because it is not
tax deductible."   Or he said, "I cannot give you
anything because I give all my offerings to the
church."   I believe this is an abomination before
God.

The tithe belongs *to God.*   You are to give it
where *He* tells you and when *He* tells you, whether
or not it is tax deductible and whether or not it is
to your church.

Of course, pastors will preach that it must all
go to the church and it must be 10 percent of the
gross.   Possibly they preach this because they are
motivated to bring the maximum amount of money
into the local church.   However, there are many
places in the Bible that significantly contradict this
interpretation—passages that these good pastors
will never show you.

One very interesting passage mentioning the tithe and what you are to do with it is found in the book of Deuteronomy:

22 "You shall surely tithe all the produce from what you sow, which comes out of the field every year.

23 "And you shall eat in the presence of the Lord your God, at the place where He chooses to establish His name, the tithe of your grain, your new wine, your oil, and the firstborn of your herd and your flock, in order that you may learn to fear the Lord your God always.

24 "And if the distance is so great for you that you are not able to bring the tithe, since the place where the Lord your God chooses to set His name is too far away from you when the Lord your God blesses you,

25 then you shall exchange it for money, and bind the money in your hand and go to the place which the Lord your God chooses.

26 "And you may spend the money for whatever your heart desires, for oxen, or sheep, or wine, or strong drink, or whatever your heart desires; and there you shall eat in the presence of the Lord your God and re-joice, you and your household. . . ."

—Deuteronomy 14

I bet that you have never heard a pastor teach on those verses. When you net it down, it says that, in some instances, God may lead you to take the tithe which belongs to Him and spend it on whatever your heart desires (according to verse 26), including wine and strong drink. *But*, you shall eat and drink this in the presence of the Lord and rejoice in the Lord while you are doing it.

The "pastors" of those days were the Levites, who performed the priestly functions for the people.

This passage in Deuteronomy goes on to say that we should take care of them:

27 "Also you shall not neglect the Levite who is in your town, for he has no portion or inheritance among you.
28 "At the end of every third year you shall bring out all the tithe of your produce in that year, and shall deposit it in your town.
29 "And the Levite, because he has no portion or inheritance among you, and the alien, the orphan and the widow who are in your town, shall come and eat and be satisfied, in order that the Lord your God may bless you in all the work of your hand which you do. . . ."
—Deuteronomy 14

These verses state that a person should bring his tithe every third year to the local priests. In a sense, you could say that this passage indicates that one-third of the tithe should go to support the local priesthood.

This concept of tithing every third year is repeated other places in Scripture:

1 "Then it shall be, when you enter the land which the Lord your God gives you as an inheritance, and you possess it and live in it,
2 that you shall take some of the first of all the produce of the ground which you shall bring in from your land that the Lord your God gives you, and you shall put it in a basket and go to the place where the Lord your God chooses to establish His name.
3 "And you shall go to the priest who is in office at that time, and say to him, 'I declare this day to the Lord my God that I have entered the land which the Lord swore to our fathers to give us.' . . .

10 'And now behold, I have brought the
first of the produce of the ground which Thou,
O Lord hast given me.' And you shall set it
down before the Lord your God, and worship
before the Lord your God;
11 and you and the Levite and the alien
who is among you shall rejoice in all the good
which the Lord your God has given you and
your household.
12 "When you have finished paying all the
tithe of your increase in the third year, the
year of tithing, then you shall give it to the
Levite, to the stranger, to the orphan and to
the widow, that they may eat in your towns,
and be satisfied.
13 "And you shall say before the Lord your
God, 'I have removed the sacred portion from
my house, and also have given it to the Levite
and the alien, the orphan and the widow,
according to all Thy commandments which
Thou has commanded me; I have not trans-
gressed or forgotten any of Thy commandments. . . .

16 "This day the Lord your God commands
you to do these statutes and ordinances. You
shall therefore be careful to do them with all
your heart and with all your soul. . . ."
—Deuteronomy 26

In no way am I trying to tell anyone how to
use his tithe or where to give it. It is God's tithe,
and He should directly tell each believer what to do
with the tithe. (A Christian needs to be faithful to
ask Him, of course, so He can and will direct him
in this matter.) However, I believe that Christians
need to break the bondage sometimes imposed upon
them by their well-meaning pastors. Sometimes
they are made to feel guilt and condemnation, if
they do not bring 10 percent of their gross income

into the church. This is simply not biblical. We are to put our tithe in a "storehouse":

> 10 "Bring the whole tithe into the storehouse, so that there may be food in My house, and test Me now in this," says the Lord of hosts, "if I will not open for you the windows of heaven, and pour out for you a blessing until it overflows. . . ."
>
> —Malachi 3

It seems that Paul looked at that "storehouse" as being personal:

> 1 Now concerning the collection for the saints, as I directed the churches of Galatia, so do you also.
> 2 On the first day of every week let each one of you put aside and save, as he may prosper, that no collections be made when I come.
>
> —1 Corinthians 16

> 1 Now concerning the collection for the saints, as I have given orders to the churches of Galatia, so you must do also:
> 2 On the first day of the week let each one of you lay something aside, storing up as he may prosper, that there be no collections when I come.
>
> —1 Corinthians 16, NKJV

There are many good ministries—such as Campus Crusade for Christ, InterVarsity Christian Fellowship, Young Life, Youth for Christ and others —that are certainly worthy of a portion of the tithe, or the Lord may lead you to give all of your tithe to your local church. This may be particularly true if it is a small, struggling church.

If I were looking at the best biblical guide for where to give our tithe it would be this verse:

6 And let the one who is taught the word share all good things with him who teaches.
—Galatians 6

This tells us to give to the one who teaches us. I believe this is talking about teaching us deep, spiritual truths. You may or may not be getting that teaching at your local church.

By writing this chapter, I am not trying to take anything away from the local church. The local church is the vehicle that God has used through the centuries, and I believe He will continue to do so. However, many local churches are selfish and are not looking to minister overseas or to aid in the outreach of other worthwhile organizations that meet needs they are not in a position to meet. Also, some local churches do not really feed and teach the flock.

You, as an individual, are the one who will ultimately have to determine where God's tithe is going to go. You must ask God and listen to Him, and then do what *He* says—nothing more and nothing less. You are the one who will have to give an account to Him as to how you dispensed His tithe.

In fact, the essence of the New Testament is that a believer should be led moment-by-moment by the Holy Spirit and not by a set of rules. This applies to every area of our lives, including finances and the tithe. When a believer makes a commitment to give say, $20 per month to a ministry, that is not a commitment until he dies. Everyone, including the ministry, realizes that such a commitment is until the Lord leads that believer to do otherwise. Some have said, "I want to support such-and-such a ministry, but I can't because I am all committed." I believe that the

Holy Spirit periodically tells a believer that it is time to reevaluate and possibly change where his tithe is going.

OFFERINGS

The tithe to God is a requirement for believers. The Bible says that we are citizens of heaven. The tithe could be thought of as the "taxes" that we pay as citizens of God's kingdom. If we do not pay our "heavenly taxes," we are "tax evaders."

If you do not pay your tithe, you are robbing God, according to what we read from Malachi 3 at the start of this chapter. If you are robbing Him, why should He bless you? As we read in Malachi, if you do not tithe, you are under a curse from God. Some of you may say that financially there is no way you could tithe. If that is your case, I have a suggestion for you.

When you get your paycheck, income tax refund or other income, cash a check for 10 percent of it and place it in an envelope. Mark on the envelope "THIS IS GOD'S MONEY" and place that envelope in a safe place. The cash is there in case you really need it. But if you take something out of that envelope, you will clearly know who you are robbing.

God will bless you if you tithe. (This includes full-time Christian workers—God did not exempt you from tithing.) God has all sorts of ways of blessing those who obey Him. For example, perhaps your car won't break down or your children's shoes will last longer. I have seen this happen. Remember the shoes of the children of Israel lasted forty years without wearing out. Try the Lord. Tithe His way and He will bless. Let me repeat the verses from Malachi on this, for they make it so clear:

8 "Will a man rob God?   Yet you are robbing Me!   But you say, 'How have we robbed
Thee?' In tithes and offerings.
9 "You are cursed with a curse, for you
are robbing Me, the whole nation of you!
10 "Bring the whole tithe into the storehouse, so that there may be food in My house,
and test Me now in this," says the Lord of
hosts, "if I will not open for you the windows
of heaven, and pour out for you a blessing
until it overflows.
11 "Then I will rebuke the devourer for
you, so that it may not destroy the fruits of
the ground; nor will your vine in the field
cast its grapes," says the Lord of hosts. . . ."

—Malachi 3

The tithe is required.   When we have given
that much, we have only done what is expected by
God.   Offerings, above and beyond the tithe, given
as an expression of love to God, come out of the
remaining 90 percent.   Actually, all of our money
belongs to God.   We need to pray to find out how
much of a love offering we can give Him.   It
pleases Him when we do so.

TITHE ON GROSS OR NET?

Many pastors emphasize that we are to tithe
on the gross income.   I do not find that in the
Bible.   The Bible simply does not say.   I feel I
should share how God has led us, although He may
not lead you the same way.   I can see the day
when our government may tax us at higher and
higher rates.   According to President Reagan, the
average U.S. citizen pays a total of 43 percent in
all taxes combined.   If this were to climb to 60, 70,
80 or 90 percent, God would not expect us to live
on nothing.   Therefore, God has led us to tithe on
the net.   Any check we receive—salary, income tax

refund or whatever—we tithe on the amount of
that check.

However, whether you tithe on the gross or
the net, be faithful to tithe. The tithe belongs to
God. Give Him what is His, and He will bless you.

A WORD TO CHURCHES
AND OTHER MINISTRIES

When the Catalina Bible Church was being
formed (where I was lay pastor for two and a half
years), the subject of financial support for the
church came up. I made the observation that it is
easy for people to discern from God when He
wants to start a church, ministry or even a
denomination, but frequently people become hard of
hearing when God tries to tell them that it is time
for that church, ministry or denomination to end.

I made reference to one very liberal denomination that was truly started under the anointing of
the Holy Spirit, but through the years it had
become so organized and structured that, when God
turned right, it was as though it kept going straight
forward—and so it has done for the last forty or
fifty years, totally apart from the Spirit and the
power of God. The reason it kept going in the
same, established direction is that there had been a
mechanism created that would continue to bring in
the finances to support it.

The other elders and I agreed that we would
let finances be the barometer in our small church.
As long as God provided the finances, we would
have a church. When He stopped providing the
finances, we would shut down the church.
Therefore, we simply had an offering box at the
back door, where people could deposit their tithes
and offerings that the Lord led them to contribute
to the church. We never took an offering and
rarely, if ever, even mentioned the offering box.

As long as I was pastor, the Lord provided amply for all of the needs.

Being on a resort island, this little church felt a need to have an outreach, so we began the "Seafarer Services" in the outdoor bowl, where people could wear their bathing suits to church and get a suntan while attending services. We brought in outstanding Christian speakers—such as Bill Bright, Ted Engstrom, Red Harper (who starred in many of the Billy Graham movies), Roy McKoewn, Josh McDowell—as well as many Hollywood stars who gave their testimony. We paid their transportation and hotel costs when they came over to minister. It was not unusual for us to have two hundred people each summer receive Jesus Christ as their personal Savior.

Here again, we only had offering boxes at the exits, and we did not take a formal offering. Some of the other people involved in the services felt that we could get 30 percent more if we took an offering. I felt that, if these outdoor services were of the Lord, He would provide the funds. And He did so, faithfully, every year.

One year, we were two hundred dollars short at the end of the summer season, when the bowl services ended. If we remained two hundred dollars short, we simply would not have them again the following season. About a week later we got a check from a mother for two hundred dollars. It turned out that her son had received Jesus Christ as his Savior there on the island, and it had totally changed his life. He had recently died, and after all expenses were paid, there were four hundred dollars left over from his life insurance. She gave two hundred dollars to his church and sent us two hundred dollars—which made us exactly break even for the summer season!

After I left the island, those in charge started taking offerings rather than simply having offering boxes at the exits. Within a year, there were not enough funds to continue the bowl services. I am not saying that every church should simply have an offering box at the back door. I do think there is a principle to be learned here.

It seems to me that what is needed is much more prayer, and much less pressure. If the group of believers, including the leaders, earnestly seek the Lord, and if the ministry or church is of Him, He *will* provide the finances to continue it. It might be well to let that be the barometer, and if the Lord stops providing funds, perhaps it is time to stop. Also, if there is a new project that the church or ministry wants to embark on, if that project is of the Lord, He will provide enough funds to do it. If it is not of Him, then let the lack of funds be an indication from the Holy Spirit that the project was not a direction that He wanted the body to take.

It is legitimate to let your needs be known, but I would question if it is of God to really put the pressure on people to give. I have seen large charismatic meetings where thirty minutes was taken to try to get a big offering. I have also seen couples out traveling and ministering, who would take thirty minutes away from the purpose that God had called them for in order to try to raise funds for their ministry. Of course, we have all seen television ministries, wherein close to half the time is spent soliciting funds.

In God's name, stop all of that nonsense! If your ministry is of God, He will provide the funds. If it is not of Him, then let it die, and move on to what God has for you. You may be part of a ministry that started under God's anointing and direction, but God may want it to end—so be sensitive. Take a minute or two to let people know what your needs are. Then pray that, if God wants you in that ministry, He will lay it on the hearts of His people to give or to send in the necessary funds. Christian ministers need to be freed from

the image of having a giant tin cup in each hand.
I do not think it is honoring to God in any way
whatsoever.

God owns the cattle on a thousand hills, and
He is certainly able to provide you with all that
you need for your church or ministry, if you trust
in Him and if you are moving in His will and His
way. If the finances run short, the thing to do is
not to spend an inordinate amount of effort to raise
funds, but instead to fall on your knees and find
out from God what you are doing wrong, and what
changes He would have you make. If you are
walking in His ways and you have needs, you should
lift up your eyes and look unto God, from whence
comes your help (Psalm 121:1,2).

However, to every believer, I would say that
we need to be equally sensitive as to where God
wants us to give our tithes and offerings. Often,
we receive and receive from a ministry or a church,
and we give nothing or little financially in return.
I believe that that is also an abomination before
God, for He loves a cheerful giver:

> 6 Now this I say, he who sows sparingly
> shall also reap sparingly; and he who sows
> bountifully shall also reap bountifully.
> 7 Let each one do just as he has purposed
> in his heart; not grudgingly or under compul-
> sion; for God loves a cheerful giver.
> —2 Corinthians 9

When you give, let it be joyfully, not grudg-
ingly. In so doing, you will be blessed abundantly.

Many people may not teach these things about
the tithe, such as using one-third of it to feed the
hungry, as well as to support the priesthood. I may
have said some things here that are different than
what you have heard before. If this chapter causes
you to examine your heart before God concerning
your giving, then I believe it has done you a

service.   However you feel about it, tithing *is in
the Bible.*

21

BEHOLD THE MOUTH

By external observation, the only thing that separates man from some of the lower primates is his speech. When God said that He made man in His own image, the unique thing that God had, which He gave to man, was speech (words).

At the judgment seat, the Bible tells us that we are going to have to give an account for all of our words—even the idle, careless words:

> **34 O generation of vipers, how can ye, being evil, speak good things? for out of the abundance of the heart the mouth speaketh.**
>
> **35 A good man out of the good treasure of the heart bringeth forth good things: and an evil man out of the evil treasure bringeth forth evil things.**
>
> **36. But I say unto you, That every idle word that men shall speak, they shall give account thereof in the day of judgment.**
>
> **37 For by thy words thou shalt be justified, and by thy words thou shalt be condemned.**
>
> **—Matthew 12, KJV**

Our words are extremely important, as Jesus tells us in these verses. We are going to have to give an account for our words on the day of judgment.

In amplifying on the importance of our words, Jesus said that if we say "yes" it should really mean *yes* and if we say "no" it should really mean *no*:

> 37   But let your communication be, Yea, yea; Nay, nay: for whatsoever is more than these cometh of evil.
>
> —Matthew 5, KJV

> 37   "But let your statement be, 'Yes, yes' or 'No, no'; and anything beyond these is of evil. . . ."
>
> —Matthew 5

Perhaps we tell our children that if they are good and clean up their room, then tomorrow we will buy them an ice cream cone. If they fulfill our request, we must be very careful to do as we have said, because our "yes" should truly mean *yes*. Similarly, if we tell someone we will teach a Sunday School class for him, or come over and help him do a particular project, we have a real obligation to be there, so that our "yes" will mean *yes*.

Children have a way of wearing down their parents. A parent may say "no" for the first nine hundred ninety-nine times but, finally, on the one thousandth time, he may simply ignore the child's disobedience. That is not letting one's "no" mean no. We have got to let it mean *no* for as many times as is necessary.

This means that if you tell someone you are going to do something, such as pick him up at 7:30, you have given your word. If you arrive at 8:30 instead, your "yes" really did not mean "yes."

In the early days of our country, a man's word was as good as his bond—just as though he had put up $5,000. In those days, suppose two men shook hands in the evening in agreement over the sale of a horse to be picked up in the morning, and both agreed that the sale was completed. If the horse died during the night, the buyer would pay the seller for the horse anyway, because he had given his word, and it was as good as a written contract.

This concept of not changing or going back on one's word is found in the Psalms:

> 1 In whose eyes a reprobate is despised,
> But who honors those who fear the
> LORD;
> He swears to his own hurt, and does
> not change; . . .
>
> —Psalm 15

This verse says that a righteous man swears to his own hurt and yet he will not change. In our example of the man buying the horse, he would not go back on his word, even though it meant financial loss to himself. Keeping your word, and letting your "yes" really mean *yes* and your "no" really mean *no*, glorifies the Lord and will stand you in good stead when you give an account of your words before the judgment seat of Christ (2 Corinthians 5:10; 1 Corinthians 3:10-15).

KEEPING AN ORAL CONTRACT

I would like to take two examples from the Old Testament of someone honoring an oral contract. One took place during the time when Joshua was conquering the land, taking captive city after city. The people of the next city that he was going to conquer had a very clever plan to avoid being wiped out by the Israelites:

> 3 When the inhabitants of Gibeon heard what Joshua had done to Jericho and to Ai,
> 4 they also acted craftily and set out as envoys, and took worn-out sacks on their don-

keys, and wineskins, worn-out and torn and mended,

5 and worn-out and patched sandals on their feet, and worn-out clothes on themselves; and all the bread of their provision was dry and had become crumbled.

6 And they went to Joshua to the camp at Gilgal, and said to him and to the men of Israel, "We have come from a far country; now therefore, make a covenant with us."

7 And the men of Israel said to the Hivites, "Perhaps you are living within our land; how then shall we make a covenant with you?"

8 But they said to Joshua, "We are your servants." The Joshua said to them, "Who are you, and where do you come from?"

9 And they said to him, "Your servants have come from a very far country because of the fame of the Lord your God; for we have heard the report of Him and all that He did in Egypt,

10 and all that He did to the two kings of the Amorites who were beyond the Jordan, to Sihon king of Heshbon and to Og king of Bashan who was at Ashtaroth.

11 "So our elders and all the inhabitants of our country spoke to us, saying, 'Take provisions in your hand for the journey, and go to meet them and say to them, "We are your servants; now then, make a covenant with us."'

12 "This our bread was warm when we took it for our provisions out of our houses on the day that we left to come to you; but now behold, it is dry and has become crumbled,

13 "And these wineskins which we filled were new, and behold, they are torn; and these our clothes and our sandals are worn out because of the very long journey."

14   So the men of Israel took some of their provisions, and did not ask for the counsel of the Lord.

15   And Joshua made peace with them and made a covenant with them, to let them live; and the leaders of the congregation swore an oath to them.

—Joshua 9

In this passage, we see that, because of the deceptive words of these people from Gideon and their worn-out sandals, clothes and so forth, the men of Israel made a peace treaty with them. But after three days, they found out they had been deceived:

16   And it came about at the end of three days after they had made a covenant with them, that they heard that they were neighbors and that they were living within their land.

17   Then the sons of Israel set out and came to their cities on the third day. Now their cities were Gibeon and Chephirah and Beeroth and Kiriath-jearim.

18   And the sons of Israel did not strike them because the leaders of the congregation had sworn to them by the Lord the God of Israel. And the whole congregation grumbled against the leaders.

19   But all the leaders said to the whole congregation, "We have sworn to them by the Lord, the God of Israel, and now we cannot touch them.

20   "This we will do to them, even let them live, lest wrath be upon us for the oath which we swore to them."

21   And the leaders said to them, "Let them live." So they became hewers of wood and

drawers of water for the whole congregation, just as the leaders had spoken to them.
—Joshua 9

Many people today would say that because this delegation from Gideon had deceived the Israelites and the peace treaty was made under false pretenses, they therefore should have voided the agreement. However, in verse 19, we see that the leaders of Israel counted their word as so important that they let these people live and assume the role of servants, rather than breaking their word.

JEPHTHAH KILLED HIS DAUGHTER

To illustrate how much keeping one's word meant in the Old Testament, especially one's word to God, let us read about what happened to Jephthah, one of the judges of Israel:

29 Now the Spirit of the Lord came upon Jephthah, so that he passed through Gilead, and from Mispah of Gilead he went on to the sons of Ammon.
30 And Jephthah made a vow to the Lord and said, "If Thou wilt indeed give the sons of Ammon into my hand,
31 then it shall be that whatever comes out of the doors of my house to meet me when I return in peace from the sons of Ammon, it shall be the Lord's, and I will offer it up as a burnt offering."
32 So Jephthah crossed over to the sons of Ammon to fight against them; and the Lord gave them into his hand.
33 And he struck them with a very great slaughter from Aroer to the entrance of Minnith, twenty cities, and as far as Abel-keramim. So the sons of Ammon were subdued before the sons of Israel.

34 When Jephthah came to his house at Mizpah, behold, his daughter was coming out to meet him with tambourines and with dancing. Now she was his one and only child; besides her he had neither son nor daughter.

35 And it came about when he saw her, that he tore his clothes and said, "Alas, my daughter! You have brought me very low, and you are among those who trouble me; for I have given my word to the Lord, and I cannot take it back."

36 So she said to him, "My father, you have given your word to the Lord; do to me as you have said, since the Lord has avenged you of your enemies, the sons of Ammon."

37 And she said to her father, "Let this thing be done for me; let me alone two months, that I may go to the mountains and weep because of my virginity, I and my companions."

38 Then he said, "Go." So he sent her away for two months; and she left with her companions, and wept on the mountains because of her virginity.

39 And it came about at the end of two months that she returned to her father, who did to her according to the vow which he had made; and she had no relations with a man. Thus it became a custom in Israel,

40 that the daughters of Israel went yearly to commemorate the daughter of Jephthah the Gileadite four days in the year.

—Judges 11

This story is almost unbelievable, that a man would sacrifice his own daughter in order to keep his word to God, but it is in the Bible.

We have just looked at one aspect of our words, primarily that of keeping our word, which would include not speaking anything that is false.

We also know that with our words we can build up or we can tear down.

YOUR MOUTH IS A TOOL OR A WEAPON

Your mouth is either a weapon that can destroy or a tool that can build. Let us first look at some examples from the Bible which inform us that the mouth can destroy:

9   With his mouth the godless man de-
     stroys his neighbor,
     But through knowledge the righteous will be
     delivered.
                                    —Proverbs 11

13   He who goes about as a talebearer
     reveals secrets,
     But he who is trustworthy conceals a
     matter.
                                    —Proverbs 11

9   He who covers a transgression seeks
     love,
     But he who repeats a matter separates
     intimate friends.
                                    —Proverbs 17

5   A false witness will not go unpunished,
     And he who tells lies will not escape.
                                    —Proverbs 19

1   . . . But a harsh word stirs up anger
                                    —Proverbs 15

28   . . . And a slanderer separates intimate
     friends.
                                    —Proverbs 16

In the preceding verses, we see that the mouth can destroy a neighbor. It can certainly destroy a neighbor's reputation. Gossips are some of the most vicious people in the world. They really kill a person's reputation, without that person being there to defend himself.

On the other hand, the mouth can be used instead to build up in a wonderful way:

> 11 The mouth of the righteous is a fountain
>   fountain of life,
>   But the mouth of the wicked conceals
>   violence.
>
> —Proverbs 10

> 3 The one who guards his mouth preserves
>   his life;
>   The one who opens wide his lips comes
>   to ruin.
>
> —Proverbs 13

> 6 Let your speech always be with grace, seasoned, as it were, with salt, so that you may know how you should respond to each person.
>
> —Colossians 4

> 31 The mouth of the righteous flows with
>   wisdom. . . .
>
> —Proverbs 10

> 18 There is one who speaks rashly like the
>   thrusts of a sword,
>   But the tongue of the wise brings heal-
>   ing. . . .

> 25 Anxiety in the heart of a man weighs it
>   down,
>   But a good work makes it glad.
>
> —Proverbs 12

1   A gentle answer turneth away wrath,
2   The tongue of the wise makes
        knowledge acceptable,

4   A soothing tongue is a tree of life, . . .

23   . . . And how delightful is a timely
        word!
                                    —Proverbs 15

24   Pleasant words are a honeycomb,
        Sweet to the soul and healing to the
        bones.
                                    —Proverbs 16

21   Death and life are in the power of the
        tongue,
        And those who love it will eat its fruit.
                                    —Proverbs 18

We want wholesome rivers of water to come
out of our mouths. We want them to be fountains
of life, don't we? Therefore, we need to guard our
mouths and not let negative things come out of
them:

1 Let not many of you become teachers,
my brethren, knowing that as such we shall
incur a stricter judgment.
2 For we all stumble in many ways. If
anyone does not stumble in what he says, he
is a perfect man, able to bridle the whole
body as well.
3 Now if we put the bits into the horses
mouths so that they may obey us, we direct
their entire body as well.
4 Behold, the ships also, though they are
so great and are driven by strong winds, are
still directed by a very small rudder, wherever
the inclination of the pilot desires.
5 So also the tongue is a small part of the
body, and yet it boasts of great things.

Behold, how great a forest is set aflame by
such a small fire!

—James 3

19 When there are many words, transgres-
       sion is unavoidable,
    But he who restrains his lips is wise.

—Proverbs 10

3 Set a guard, O Lord, over my mouth;
    Keep watch over the door of my lips.

—Psalm 141

29 Let no unwholesome word proceed from
your mouth, but only such a word as is good
for edification according to the need of the
moment, that it may give grace to those who
hear.

—Ephesians 4

20 Do you see a man who is hasty in his
       words?
    There is more hope for a fool than for
       him.

—Proverbs 29

6 "Listen, for I shall speak noble things;
    And the opening of my lips will produce
       right things.
7 "For my mouth will utter truth;
    And wickedness is an abomination to my
       lips. . . ."

—Proverbs 8

23 He who guards his mouth and his
       tongue,
    Guards his soul from troubles.

—Proverbs 21

Our mouths are so very powerful. Some day,
according to the Bible, we are going to have to

give an account for all of our words. We may not like the fact that we are going to be judged on our words but, believe it or not, *it is in the Bible.*

22

JUSTICE IN THE BIBLE

The justice system in the United States is based solely on punishment. If somebody steals a car and wrecks it, he is punished by spending time in prison. If someone commits some lesser crime, he is punished accordingly. If someone is guilty of rape and murder, he is sent to prison and, in some cases, actually executed.

One of the weaknesses of this system of punishment is "victim's rights." There are groups springing up all over trying to help the victims of various crimes to have some rights in the process. However, our system esentially ignores the victim and tries only to punish the offender.

In the Bible, the system of justice outlined in the Old Testament is quite different. It is primarily based on *restitution*. In fact, if someone in those days were to steal an animal and kill it or sell it, he would frequently have to pay back double or even four or five times what he stole. For example, in the verses below, if a man steals a sheep and sells or slaughters it, he must pay back four sheep for the one sheep he stole from the victim:

1 "If a man steals an ox or a sheep, and slaughters it or sells it, he shall pay five oxen for the ox and four sheep for the sheep.
2 "If the thief is caught while breaking in, and is struck so that he dies, there will be no bloodguiltiness on his account.
3 "But if the sun has risen on him, there will be blood-guiltiness on his account. He shall surely make restitution; if he owns nothing, then he shall be sold for his theft.
4 "If what he stole is actually found alive in his possession, whether an ox or a donkey or a sheep, he shall pay double. . . ."

—Exodus 22

The same thing is true concerning stealing money or goods. The thief has to pay back double the amount that he stole:

7 "If a man gives his neighbor money or goods to keep for him, and it is stolen from the man's house, if the thief is caught, he shall pay double. . . ."

—Exodus 22

If a man borrows someone else's horse or cow or something else, and it is injured or dies while he has it, then he has to make full restitution:

14 "And if a man borrows anything from his neighbor, and it is injured or dies while its owner is not with it, he shall make full restitution.
15 "If its owner is with it, he shall not make restitution; if it is hired, it came for its hire. . . ."

—Exodus 22

We could proceed with more examples, but you get the idea from these that the biblical basis of justice was primarily restitution. If we had that type of system in America today, and someone stole someone's car and wrecked it, that individual would have had to work until he could buy two cars of that same value to pay back the victim of his crime. There would be a lot less car theft going on, if this were the case. A one-year suspended sentence without restitution does not help the victim and it does not really punish the offender. Working to buy the victim two comparable cars would both help the victim and also be a real lesson to the offender.

THE DEATH PENALTY
FOR SEXUAL SINS, MURDER AND . . .

In the Old Testament system of justice, in some case, wherein restitution was not possible, the penalty was death. This was particularly true for many sexual sins:

> 19 "Whoever lies with an animal shall surely be put to death. . . ."
> —Exodus 22

> 22 "If a man is found lying with a married woman, then both of them shall die, the man who lay with the woman, and the woman; thus, you shall purge the evil from Israel. . . ."
> —Deuteronomy 22

> 25 "But if in the field the man finds the girl who is engaged, and the man forces her and lies with her, then only the man who lies with her shall die. . . ."
> —Deuteronomy 22

> 10 'If there is a man who commits adultery with another man's wife, one who commits

adultery with his friend's wife, the adulterer
and the adulteress shall surely be put to death.

11 'If there is a man who lies with his
father's wife, he has uncovered his father's
nakedness; both of them shall surely be put to
death, their bloodguiltiness is upon them.

12 'If there is a man who lies with his
daughter-in-law, both of them shall surely be
put to death; they have committed incest, their
bloodguiltiness is upon them.

13 'If there is a man who lies with a male
as those who lie with a woman, both of them
have committed a detestable act; they shall
surely be put to death. Their bloodguiltiness
is upon them.

14 'If there is a man who marries a woman
and her mother, it is immorality; both he and
they shall be burned with fire, that there may
be no immorality in your midst.

15 'If there is a man who lies with an
animal, he shall surely be put to death; you
shall also kill the animal.

16 'If there is a woman who approaches any
animal to mate with it, you shall kill the woman and the animal; they shall surely be put
to death. Their bloodguiltiness is upon them. . . .'

—Leviticus 20

For various sexual sins, mentioned in the
preceding verses, the penalty was death. There was
also a death penalty for sacrificing to any god
other than Jehovah God of the Old Testament:

20 "He who sacrifices to any god, other
than to the Lord alone, shall be utterly destroyed. . . ."

—Exodus 22

2 "If there is found in your midst, in any
of your towns, which the Lord your God is

giving you, a man or a woman who does what is evil in the sight of the Lord your God, by transgresing His covenant,

3 and has gone and served other gods and worshiped them, or the sun or the moon or any of the heavenly host, which I have not commanded,

4 and if it is told you and you have heard of it, then you shall inquire thoroughly. And behold, if it is true and the thing certain that this detestable thing has been done in Israel,

5 then you shall bring out that man or that woman who has done this evil deed, to your gates, that is, the man or the woman, and you shall stone them to death.

6 "On the evidence of two witnesses or three witnesses, he who is to die shall be put to death; he shall not be put to death on the evidence of one witness.

7 "The hand of the witnesses shall be first against him to put him to death, and afterward the hand of all the people. So you shall purge the evil from your midst. . . ."

—Deuteronomy 17

In the Old Testament, murder also automatically brought the death penalty:

16 'But if he struck him down with an iron object, so that he died, he is a murderer; the murderer shall surely be put to death.

17 'And if he struck him down with a stone in the hand, by which he may die, and as a result he died, he is a murderer; the murderer shall surely be put to death.

18 'Or if he struck him with a wooden object in the hand, by which he may die, and as a result he died, he is a murderer; the murderer shall surely be put to death.

19 'The blood avenger himself shall put the murderer to death; he shall put him to death when he meets him.

20 'And if he pushed him of hatred, or threw something at him lying in wait and as a result he died,

21 or if he struck him down with his hand in enmity, and as a result he died, the one who struck him shall surely be put to death, he is a murderer; the blood avenger shall put the murderer to death when he meets him. . . .'

—Numbers 35

A very interesting thing to note is that in the Old Testament, juvenile delinquency was also punishable by death. If a son absolutely refused to obey his father, then he was to suffer the death penalty:

18 "If any man has a stubborn and rebellious son who will not obey his father or his mother, and when they chastise him, he will not even listen to them.

19 then his father and mother shall seize him, and bring him out to the elders of his city at the gateway of his home town.

20 "And they shall say to the elders of his city, 'This son of ours is stubborn and rebellious, he will not obey us, he is a glutton and a drunkard.'

21 "Then all the men of his city shall stone him to death; so you shall remove the evil from your midst, and all Israel shall hear of it and fear. . . ."

—Deuteronomy 21

Consequently, the nation of Israel did not have any juvenile delinquents, street gangs or young "punks" roving the streets.

OTHER PUNISHMENTS

While other punishments for crimes are rare in the Bible, there are few. Here are two of the more drastic ones:

> 1 "If there is a dispute between men and they go to court, and the judges decide their case, and they justify the righteous and condemn the wicked,
> 2 then it shall be if the wicked man deserves to be beaten, the judge shall then make him lie down and be beaten in his presence with the number of stripes according to his guilt.
> 3 "He may beat him forty times but no more, lest he beat him with many more stripes than these, and your brother be degraded in your eyes. . . ."
>
> —Deuteronomy 25

> 11 "If two men, a man and his countryman, are struggling together, and the wife of one comes near to deliver her husband from the hand of the one who is striking him, and puts out her hand and seizes his genitals,
> 12 then you shall cut off her hand; you shall not show pity. . . ."
>
> —Deuteronomy 25

Cutting off someone's hand seems a gruesome and drastic punishment, but it is in the Bible.

RESTORATION, DEATH AND SACRIFICE

We see that the Old Testament system of justice was primarily based on restitution, the offender frequently having to pay back double or even up to five times the amount stolen. Thus, the victims of the crime had incredible rights in biblical times. In other cases, where restitution was not possible—such as in rape, adultery, sex with an animal or murder—the death penalty was the sentence. In cases where the death penalty was required, this of course was punishment and not restitution. So really the Old Testament system of justice was primarily restitution, for civil crimes, along with some punishment, especially the death penalty, for capital crimes. There were no suspended sentences nor paroles.

Frequently, in addition to restitution for various sins, the people in the Old Testament were required to make sacrifices to God to atone for their sins (Leviticus 4:35).

This is the system of justice that is described in the Old Testament. It might be well for the United States and other countries to evaluate their entire justice systems to see if God may not have designed a better way. You may not think it was a very good system, but it *is* in the Bible.

23

NUCLEAR WINTER

Scientists have put forth a theory regarding what is commonly referred to as "nuclear winter." This theory proposes that if there were an all-out nuclear war, there would be so much debris blown into the atmosphere that it would cut out the sunlight to the extent that we would have a permanent winter.

In the first place, if God wanted to do so, He could cause a rain that would precipitate all the particles in the atmosphere:

> 8 The earth quaked;
> The heavens also dropped rain at the
> presence of God;
> Sinai itself quaked at the presence of
> God, the God of Israel.
> 9 Thou didst shed abroad a plentiful rain,
> O God;
> Thou didst confirm Thine inheritance,
> when it was parched.
> 10 Thy creatures settled in it;
> Thou didst provide in Thy goodness for
> the poor, O God.
> —Psalm 68

In looking at a possible nuclear winter, we first need to realize that it was God who created the seasons:

> 17 Thou has established all the boundaries
> of the earth;
> Thou hast made summer and winter.
> —Psalm 74

Going beyond that, we see that God Himself guaranteed that the seasons would continue, as long as the earth exists:

> 21 And the Lord smelled the soothing aroma; and the Lord said to Himself, "I will never again curse the ground on account of man, for the intent of man's heart is evil from his youth; and I will never again destroy every living thing, as I have done.
> 22 "While the earth remains,
> Seedtime and harvest,
> And cold and heat,
> And summer and winter,
> And day and night
> Shall not cease."
> —Genesis 8

Since God created the seasons, He can certainly maintain them. According to what we just read, God has promised that seedtime and harvest, winter *and* summer, cold *and* heat would never cease. Therefore, we know that there will never be a nuclear winter. It is in the Bible.

24

CHRISTMAS MYTHS

Some of what people believe about the Bible is purely fiction and has grown out of folklore or tradition from the past.

For example, one such belief that people hold is that, when the angels appeared to the shepherds who were in the field, they sang to them. Yet there is no evidence to support this concept:

8 And in the same region there were some shepherds staying out in the fields, and keeping watch over their flock by night.

9 And an angel of the Lord suddenly stood before them, and the glory of the Lord shone around them; and they were terribly frightened.

10 And the angel said to them, "Do not be afraid; for behold, I bring you good news of a great joy which shall be for all the people;

11 for today in the city of David there has been born for you a Savior, who is Christ the Lord.

12 "And this will be a sign for you: you will find a baby wrapped in cloths, and lying in a manger."

13 And suddenly there appeared with the

angel a multitude of the heavenly host praising
God, and saying,
14   "Glory to God in the highest,
     And on earth peace among men with
     whom He is pleased."

—Luke 2

In this passage, we see that the primary angel
in verse 10 "*said*" something to the shepherds.
Then verse 13 says that the host of angels were
praising God and "*saying.*"

Also, we know that the "wise men" (magi)
—however many there were (the Bible does not
say that there were three)—did *not* come to Christ
when He was in the manger in the stable. They
came to Him much later, when He was living in a
"house":

1 Now after Jesus was born in Bethlehem
of Judea in the days of Herod the king,
behold, magi from the east arrived in Jerusalem, saying,
2 "Where is He who has been born King of
the Jews?   For we saw His star in the east,
and have come to worship Him."
3 And when Herod the king heard it, he
was troubled and all Jerusalem with him.
4 And gathering together all the chief
priests and scribes of the people, he began to
inquire of them where the Christ was to be
born.
5 And they said to him, "In Bethlehem of
Judea, for so it has been written by the
prophet,
6 'AND YOU, BETHLEHEM, LAND OF
     JUDAH,
   ARE BY NO MEANS LEAST AMONG THE
     LEADERS OF JUDAH;
   FOR OUT OF YOU SHALL COME
     FORTH A RULER,

WHO WILL SHEPHERD MY PEOPLE
ISRAEL.'"

7 Then Herod secretly called the magi, and
ascertained from them the time the star appeared.

8 And he sent them to Bethlehem, and
said, "Go and make careful search for the
Child; and when you have found Him, report to
me, that I too may come and worship Him."

9 And having heard the king, they went
their way; and lo, the star, which they had
seen in the east, went on before them, until it
came and stood over where the Child was.

10 And when they saw the star, they rejoiced exceedingly with great joy.

11 And they came into the house and saw
the Child with Mary His mother; and they fell
down and worshiped Him; and opening their
treasures they presented to Him gifts of gold
and frankincense and myrrh.

12 And having been warned by God in a
dream not to return to Herod, they departed
for their own country by another way.

—Matthew 2

In verse 11, we see that the wise men came to
the "house" where the Child was, and they (however
many there were) gave Him three different kinds of
gifts—gold, frankincense and myrrh. There could
have been two magi or ten bringing Him these three
types of gifts.

Back in verse 7, we see that Herod wanted to
find out from these wise men (magi) when the star
had appeared, because they had observed it when
they were back in the "east," which most likely was
Ur of the Chaldees. Evidently, it would have taken
them some time to make preparations for that long
a journey (perhaps a year or so). Also, to have
come all the way from the "east" would have taken

awhile. By the time they got to Bethlehem, Mary and Jesus were living in a house.

The magi must have told Herod that the star appeared about a year or a year and a half before, because Herod had all of the babies killed that were two years old and under:

13 Now when they had departed, behold, an angel of the Lord appeared to Joseph in a dream, saying, "Arise and take the Child and His mother, and flee to Egypt, and remain there until I tell you; for Herod is going to search for the Child to destroy Him."

14 And he arose and took the Child and His mother by night, and departed for Egypt;

15 and was there until the death of Herod, that what was spoken by the Lord through the prophet might be fulfilled, saying, "OUT OF EGYPT DID I CALL MY SON."

16 Then when Herod saw that he had been tricked by the magi, he became very enraged, and sent and slew all the male children who were in Bethlehem and in all its environs, from two years old and under, according to the time which he had ascertained from the magi.

—Matthew 2

ANOTHER MYTH ABOUT JESUS

As we mentioned in Chapter 1, Jesus is never referred to as the "lily of the valley" or "the rose of Sharon." In the Bible, these are terms used for a beautiful black lady that King Solomon was marrying. Here are some of the things that this lady had to say:

2 "May he kiss me with the kisses of his mouth!
For your love is better than wine.

3 "Your oils have a pleasing fragrance,
Your name is like purified oil;
Therefore the maidens love you.
4 "Draw me after you and let us run
together!
The king has brought me into his
chambers." . . .

5 "I am black but lovely
O daughters of Jerusalem,
Like the tents of Kedar,
Like the curtains of Solomon. . . .

12 "While the king was at his table,
My perfume gave forth its fragrance.
13 "My beloved is to me a pouch of myrrh
Which lies all night between my
breasts.
14 "My beloved is to me a cluster of
henna blossoms
In the vineyards of Engedi." . . .
16 "How handsome you are, my beloved,
And so pleasant!
Indeed our couch is luxuriant!
17 "The beams of our houses are cedars,
Our rafters, cypresses.
—Song of Solomon 1

1 "I am the rose of Sharon,
The lily of the valleys."
—Song of Solomon 2

It is this woman in the Song of Solomon who
refers to herself as "the lily of the valleys" and the
"rose of Sharon." Later Solomon responds to her
by saying this:

3 "Your lips are like a scarlet thread,
And your mouth is lovely.
Your temples are like a slice of a
pomegranate
Behind your veil.

> 4   "Your neck is like the tower of David
>   Built with rows of stones,
>   On which are hung a thousand shields,
>   All the round shields of the mighty men.
> 5   "Your two breasts are like two fawns,
>   Twins of a gazelle,
>   Which feed among the lilies.
> 6   "Until the cool of the day
>   When the shadows flee away,
>   I will go my way to the mountain of
>   myrrh
>   And to the hill of frankincense.
> 7   "You are altogether beautiful,
>   my darling,
>   And there is no blemish in you. . . ."
>   —Song of Solomon 4

The breaks in the book of the Song of Solomon, as to who was speaking in the various verses, are according to the *Ryrie Study Bible* (helps by Charles Caldwell Ryrie, Th.D., Ph.D., Chairman, Department of Systematic Theology, Dallas Theological Seminary).

In contrast to being lovely and beautiful, the Bible says of Jesus that His appearance was such that we should not be attracted to Him:

> 2   For He grew up before Him like a ten-
>   der shoot,
>   And like a root out of parched ground;
>   He has no stately form or majesty
>   That we should look upon Him,
>   Nor appearance that we should be
>   attracted to Him.
> 3   He was despised and forsaken of men,
>   A man of sorrows, and acquainted with
>   grief;
>   And like one from whom men hide their
>   face,
>   He was despised, and we did not esteem
>   Him.

4   Surely our griefs He Himself bore,
     And our sorrows He carried;
     Yet we ourselves esteemed Him stricken,
     Smitten of God, and afflicted.

5   But He was pierced through for our
         transgressions,
     He was crushed for our iniquities;
     The chastening for our well-being fell
         upon Him,
     And by His scourging we are healed.
6   All of us like sheep have gone astray,
     Each of us has turned to his own way;
     But the Lord has caused the iniquity of
         us all
     To fall on Him.
7   He was oppressed and He was afflicted,
     Yet He did not open His mouth;
     Like a lamb that is led to slaughter,
     And like a sheep that is silent before
         its shearers,
     So He did not open His mouth.
8   By oppression and judgment He was
         taken away;
     And as for His generation, who
         considered
     That He was cut off out of the land of
         the living,
     For the transgression of my people to
         whom the stroke was due?
9   His grave was assigned with wicked
         men,
     Yet He was with a rich man in His
         death,
     Because He had done no violence,
     Nor was there any deceit in His mouth.
                                —Isaiah 53

     We are certainly grateful that, as it says in
verses 4 and 5 of Isaiah 53, Jesus Christ has borne

our sorrows and was killed for our iniquities and transgressions. This prophecy was made hundreds of years before Jesus was born, yet I am convinced that it describes Him perfectly.

Before we leave our discussion of the Song of Solomon, we should mention that there are some theologians who would say that this is a picture of Christ and the church. I would have to take exception to that. There are too many things that do not fit. For example, if this were a picture of Christ and the church, Christ would first have intercourse with the church, then subsequently desert the church. Chapter 5 says this:

> 2   "I was asleep, but my heart was awake.
>   A voice! My beloved was knocking:
>   'Open to me, my sister, my darling,
>   My dove, my perfect one!
>   For my head is drenched with dew,
>   My locks with the damp of the night.'
> 3   "I have taken off my dress,
>   How can I put it on again?
>   I have washed my feet,
>   How can I dirty them again?
> 4   "My beloved extended his hand through
>   the opening,
> 5   "I arose to open to my beloved;
>   And my hands dripped with myrrh,
>   And my fingers with liquid myrrh
>   On the handles of the bolt.
> 6   "I opened to my beloved,
>   But my beloved had turned away and
>   had gone!
>   My heart went out to him as he spoke.
>   I searched for him, but I did not find
>   him;
>   I called him, but he did not answer me.
> 7   "The watchmen who make the rounds in
>   the city found me,
>   They struck me and wounded me;

The guardsmen of the walls took away
my shawl from me.
8   "I adjure you, O daughters of Jerusalem,
If you find my beloved,
As to what you will tell him:
For I am lovesick."

—Song of Solomon 5

In these verses, we see that Solomon deserted his black bride. If theologians are going to try to make Solomon and this black lady a picture of Jesus and His bride, they need to be consistent all the way through. There is absolutely no way that Jesus is going to abandon the church and then the church go out desperately searching for Him. To attempt to make Solomon a type of Christ (which he definitely is not) is stretching the Scriptures way beyond capacity.

The book of "The Song of Solomon" is simply a beautiful story about the spiritual and physical love between a man and a woman. It describes in detail their enjoyment of each other's bodies. The theologians who cannot handle beautiful, God-ordained sex—even if it is recorded in the Bible—are the ones who try to make this book into a Messianic prophecy.

There are many very valid Messianic prophecies in the Old Testament, which require no distortion of the meaning of the passage in order to be prophetic of the coming Messiah. Since there are enough of these legitimate prophecies about Jesus, I see no reason to try to stretch this book to try to make it more than it was meant to be.

He was born in order to die in our place. This is why the celebration of Christmas and Easter are inseparable. You cannot have one without the other. Not only was He born, but He also died for *our* sins. But the really exciting part is that He rose again! He demonstrated victory over death and the grave, a victory that He has also made available to us through belief in Him.

In this chapter we have examined just a few common misconceptions that are frequently assumed to be based on the Bible. None of these are of any major significance; so you might legitimately ask, "Why bring it up?" The reason I include this chapter is to help you realize how easy it is to attribute certain teachings or ideas to the Bible that, in fact, are not even there. This may be due to what you were taught as a child, something you heard in Sunday School, songs you have sung or what others have said. Perhaps you have never really checked these things out for yourself in the Bible.

The point is that it is important to read the Bible for yourself to see what it truly has to say, rather than letting your knowledge about it be solely dependent on heresay. It is really a terrific book. Try it—you'll like it.

The Bible claims that Jesus Christ is alive, that He rose from the dead. In fact, when forming a company, one Christian put on the papers that Jesus Christ was the president. The state office said, "We're sorry. It has to be a living person." He then stated that Jesus Christ *was* alive. An interesting discussion then ensued.

However, the resurrection of Jesus Christ is very different from reincarnation, as we will see in the next chapter.

25

REINCARNATION

There are many religions in the world which teach that if we live a good life, we will come back in a different body for another life. If we have lived a very good life, they teach that we will come back into a higher and nicer level of life. If we have lived an evil or bad life, we will come in a lower level of life. Some even teach that we could come back in the form of animals. Of course, in one short chapter we cannot discuss this subject in depth. Our intent here is to concentrate on what the Bible has to say about it. Reincarnation is totally opposed to all of the teachings in the Scriptures. One of the basic tenets of both the Old and New Testaments is the resurrection of the dead at the end of the age, wherein every soul will be united with his body. Obviously, if this is going to happen, a soul could not be reunited with twenty or thirty different bodies. In fact, one of the basic foundational truths of Christianity is that Jesus Christ rose from the dead and reunited with His body and that, because of this, we Christians can have hope that we too will experience the resurrection:

> 12 Now if Christ is preached, that He has been raised from the dead, how do some among

you say that there is no resurrection of the dead?

13 But if there is no resurrection of the dead, not even Christ has been raised;

14 and if Christ has not been raised, then our preaching is vain, your faith also is vain.

15 Moreover we are even found to be false witnesses of God, because we witnessed against God that He raised Christ, whom He did not raise, if in fact the dead are not raised.

16 For if the dead are not raised, not even Christ has been raised;

17 and if Christ has not been raised, your faith is worthless; you are still in your sins.

18 Then those also who have fallen asleep in Christ have perished.

19 If we have hoped in Christ in this life only, we are of all men most to be pitied.

20 But now Christ has been raised from dead, the first fruits of those who are asleep.

—1 Corinthians 15

As you can see from the passage above, if there is no resurrection of the dead, then Christians are to be pitied and their faith is absolutely worthless. The Christian faith depends entirely upon the resurrection of Jesus Christ from the dead and His promise that at the end of the age He would raise His followers. This means reuniting their souls with their bodies in the grave and raising them back to life.

40 "For this is the will of My Father, that everyone who beholds the Son and believes in Him, may have eternal life; and I Myself will raise him up on the last day."

44 "No one can come to Me, unless the Father who sent Me draws him; and I will raise him up on the last day. . . ."

—John 6

PULLING BACK THE CURTAIN OF DEATH

There is only one place in the Bible where the curtain of death is pulled back and we can catch a glimpse of what occurs on the other side of death. This was a story told by Jesus Christ and, if anyone knew what was on the other side of death, certainly He did, coming down from heaven as He did. We know that this is not a parable, because Jesus never used proper names in parables. He graciously left out the proper name of the rich man, but he included the proper name of the beggar, in the event which He described:

19 "Now there was a certain rich man, and he habitually dressed in purple and fine linen, gaily living in splendor every day.

20 "And a certain poor man named Lazarus was laid at his gate, covered with sores,

21 and longing to be fed with the crumbs which were falling from the rich man's table; besides, even the dogs were coming and licking his sores.

22 "Now it came about that the poor man died and he was carried away by the angels to Abraham's bosom; and the rich man also died and was buried.

23 "And in Hades he lifted up his eyes, being in torment and saw Abraham far away, and Lazarus in his bosom.

24 "And he cried out and said, 'Father Abraham, have mercy on me, and send Lazarus, that he may dip the tip of his finger in water and cool off my tongue; for I am in agony in this flame.'

25 "But Abraham said, 'Child, remember that during your life you received your good things, and likewise Lazarus bad things; but now he is being comforted here, and you are in agony.

26 'And besides all this, between us and
you there is a great chasm fixed, in order that
those who wish to come over from here to you
may not be able, and that none may cross over
from there to us.'
27 "And he said, 'Then I beg you, Father,
that you send him to my father's house—
28 for I have five brothers—that he may
warn them, lest they also come to this place
of torment.'
29 "But Abraham said, 'They have Moses
and the Prophets; let them hear them.'
30 "But he said, 'No, Father Abraham, but
if someone goes to them from the dead, they
will repent!'
31 "But he said to him, 'If they do not
listen to Moses and the Prophets, neither will
they be persuaded if someone rises from the
dead.'"

—Luke 16

In that actual event that Jesus Christ
describes here, we see that each soul remains intact
and uniquely identified. He also informs us that
there is an impassable chasm between Hades, where
the rich man was, and the place where Abraham and
Lazarus were.   Hebrews overtly states that no soul
can cross back into the land of the living again:

27 And inasmuch as it is appointed for men
to die once and after this comes judgment, . . ."

—Hebrews 9

This verse from the letter to the Hebrews
states that a man dies *once*.   After he dies, the
next event that comes in his life after death is the
judgment before God Almighty and His Son, Jesus
Christ.   If one believes the Scriptures, this verse
totally excludes multiple deaths, because each man
is going to die only one time.

However, the important thing is that after we die, we must all eventually stand before the judgment seat of God. This is going to be an awesome experience. The Bible describes this event to us as follows:

> 11 And I saw a great white throne and Him who sat upon it, from whose presence earth and heaven fled away, and no place was found for them.
>
> 12 And I saw the dead, the great and the small, standing before the throne, and books were opened; and another book was opened, which is the book of life; and the dead were judged from the things which were written in the books, according to their deeds.
>
> 13 And the sea gave up the dead which were in it, and death and Hades gave up the dead which were in them; and they were judged, every one of them according to their deeds.
>
> 14 And death and Hades were thrown into the lake of fire.
>
> 15 And if anyone's name was not found written in the book of life, he was thrown into the lake of fire.
>
> —Revelation 20

According to this, every individual—including those who were buried at sea and whose bodies have spread out into a million molecules—is going to be raised up, his soul reunited with his body, and he will stand before God. The main criterion at this final judgment is going to be whether one's name is written in the book of life. If it is, he is destined for eternal life. If it is not, he is going to be thrown into a lake of fire which lasts forever.

Although it is not the most pleasant subject, let's first read about the torment of the lake of

fire. This is something that the Bible clearly
teaches:

> 10 And the devil who deceived them was
> thrown into the lake of fire and brimstone,
> where the beast and the false prophet are
> also; and they will be tormented day and night
> forever and ever. . . .
> 14 And death and Hades were thrown into
> the lake of fire. This is the second death, the
> lake of fire.
> 15 And if anyone's name was not found
> written in the book of life, he was thrown
> into the lake of fire.
>
> —Revelation 20

This passage tells us that those thrown into
the lake of fire will be tormented day and night,
and this includes the devil. Those who are
worshiping the devil are going to lose in the end.

This torment is discussed again concerning
those who take on the mark of the beast at the
end of this age:

> 9 And another angel, a third one, followed
> them, saying with a loud voice, "If anyone
> worships the beast and his image, and receives
> a mark on his forehead or upon his hand,
> 10 he also will drink of the wine of the
> wrath of God, which is mixed in full strength
> in the cup of His anger; and he will be
> tormented with fire and brimstone in the
> presence of the holy angels and in the pre-
> sence of the Lamb.
> 11 And the smoke of their torment goes up
> forever and ever; and they have no rest day
> and night, those who worship the beast and
> his image, and whoever receives the mark of
> his name."
>
> —Revelation 14

Here we see that this torment goes on day and night forever. Some would say that this condition of being in the lake of fire is a temporary one, but the Bible clearly states that this torment will continue forever, without rest.

According to the Bible, there is no reincarnation. There is no second chance. If our names are written in the book of life, we will spend eternity on the glorious new earth that God is going to create. If our names are not written in the book of life, then we will spend eternity in the lake of fire.

THE BOOK OF LIFE

A very critical question then arises: How do we get our names written in the book of life? To be honest, the Bible does not explicitly give us a great deal of information about this. However, it does give us some significant clues:

1 Therefore, my beloved brethren whom I long to see, my joy and crown, so stand firm in the Lord, my beloved.
2 I urge Euodia and I urge Syntyche to live in harmony in the Lord.
3 Indeed, true comrade, I ask you also to help these women who have shared my struggle in the cause of the gospel, together with Clement also, and the rest of my fellow workers, whose names are in the book of life.
4 Rejoice in the Lord always; again I will say, rejoice!

—Philippians 4

Here Paul is writing to the Christians at Philippi. In verse 1, he calls them "brothers," and he tells them to stand firm in the "Lord," which is Jesus Christ. He further says that these are people whose names are written in the book of life (verse 3).

Brethren (brothers) in the New Testament refers to those who have invited Jesus Christ to be their Savior and Lord (Master). These are the ones whose names are written in the book of life.

SUMMARY AND CONCLUSION

We have seen that, according to the Bible, we are to die one time. Ultimately our bodies are to be resurrected and our souls reunited with them, just as Jesus rose from the dead and His soul was reunited with His resurrected body.

Since the resurrection of Jesus Christ is the foundational truth of the Scriptures, if He did not rise from the dead, then Easter is false and Christianity is false. Since the resurrection is such a key subject—indeed, the pivotal point on which all of Christianity rests—it merits a closer examination with an open mind.

26

EVIDENCES
OF THE RESURRECTION

I invite you, in this chapter, to objectively consider with me the evidence concerning the resurrection from the dead of Jesus Christ. Upon examining the evidence, it becomes apparent that no one denies that He was a living being who walked the earth almost two thousand years ago. During His tenure on earth, He made such claims as these:

1. "If you believe in me, I will give you eternal life."

2. "If you ask me, I will forgive your sins."

3. "Ask anything in my name and I will give it to you."

4. "No man can come to God except by me."

If any of the religious leaders of today were to make a single one of these claims, we would consider him a lunatic or a super con artist. The only other alternative is that the individual who made these claims was actually God in human form and could back them up.

Jesus Christ stated that in order to prove that He was God, and that these claims were true, He would bring Himself back to life after being executed and remaining in the grave for three days and three nights. Therefore, Christianity must stand or fall based on whether or not its leader experienced a resurrection.

Some people might say that He was a wonderful teacher, the best man who ever lived (but not God), or a good example to follow. However, the claims that He made do not allow us this option. He was either God and capable of fulfilling His claims, or He was a lunatic or something worse. This is a binary decision; there is no third option. He was either God *or* false and evil. The decision as to who He was is contingent upon whether or not Jesus experienced a resurrection.

It is interesting to note that the New Testament states this:

> **14** and if Christ has not been raised, then our preaching is vain, your faith also is vain.
> **15** Moreover we are even found to be false witnesses of God, because we witnessed against God that He raised Christ, whom He did not raise, if in fact the dead are not raised.
> **16** For if the dead are not raised, not even Christ has been raised;
> **17** and if Christ has not been raised, your faith is worthless; you are still in your sins.
> **18** Then those also who have fallen asleep in Christ have perished.
> **19** If we have hoped in Christ in this life only, we are of all men most to be pitied.
> —1 Corinthians 15

It states here that if Christ is not raised from the dead, the Christians are to be pitied above all people on earth. On the other hand, it would be logical to assume that if He did rise from the dead, then the people who do not believe are to be the most pitied. Since the resurrection is the key, pivotal question, let's now take a look at the evidence in the case.

THE DOCUMENTS

The documents which we will use for our analysis are four books contained in the New Testament. We will use Matthew, Mark, Luke and John, since they give a detailed account of the life, death and alleged resurrection of Jesus Christ. We will not even assume that you believe that these letters were inspired by God. Logically, we have two choices in examining them. There were either written as documents recounting events which actually happened, or they are fiction.

If they are fiction, we have two further choices for our perusal:

1. These fictional works were written completely independently of one another.

2. These fictional works were written in collusion in an attempt to deceive.

There are intellectual difficulties with either of these positions. The four documents are far too similar to have been written completely independently of each other. No thinking man would attempt to defend that position, after examing them. The other possibility, assuming they are fiction, is that they are part of a deceptive plot. This position also presents several difficulties, since they are too dissimilar to have been written simultaneously; there are even apparent contradictions among them. Further, as we will see later, most of the authors of these documents were willing to be executed rather than to renounce their validity.

Since the assumption that these documents are fictional presents serious difficulties, let us turn our attention to the possibility that they actually record events that did occur at a point in time.

The account of an eye witness is readily distinguishable from the account of one who is merely retelling what others have told him. Anyone who is accustomed to weighing evidence in court or in historical study soon learns how to distinquish the report of an eye witness from mere heresay evidence. Any careful student of the Gospel records of the resurrection will readily detect many marks of the eye witness.

Some years ago, when Dr. Reuben A. Torrey was lecturing at an American university, a gentleman was introduced to him as a skeptic. He asked him, "What line of study are you pursuing?" He replied that he was pursuing a post-graduate course in history with a view to a professorship in history. Dr. Torrey said, "Then you know that the account of an eye witness differs in marked respects from the account of one who is simply telling what he has heard from others?" "Yes," he replied. Dr. Torrey next asked, "Have you carefully read the four Gospel accounts of the resurrection of Christ?" He replied, "I have." "Tell me, have you not noticed clear indications that they were derived from eye witnesses?" "Yes" he replied, "I have been greatly struck by this in reading the accounts." Anyone who carefully and intelligently reads them will be struck with the same fact.

Wilhelm DeWette, one of the great leaders of rationalism, gave the claim of Christ's resurrection the most precise, scientific investigation. He concluded: "The resurrection of Jesus Christ cannot be called into doubt any more than the historical certainty of the assassination of Caesar."

Even that is an understatement, because we do not have the testimony of any eye witnesses who saw the assassination of Caesar or who attended his funeral. Not one. But we do possess the statements of such men as Matthew, John and Peter, truthful witnesses who actually saw the risen Christ and heard Him speak.

It is well known that Lord Lyttleton and his friend Gilbert West left Oxford University at the close of an academic year, each determined to give attention during the long vacation to the conversion of Paul and the resurrection of Christ, in order to prove the "baselessness of both."

They met again in the autumn and compared experiences. Lord Lyttleton had become convinced of the truth of Paul's conversion and Gilbert West of the resurrection of Jesus Christ. Said West: "As I have studied the evidence of the resurrection of Jesus Christ from the dead and have weighed it according to the laws of evidence, I have become satisfied that Jesus really rose from the dead as recorded in the Gospels. I have written my book on that side—the side of Christ and His truth."

If the reader of this work has not personally examined the New Testament and, as an adult, read at least the four letters under consideration, then it would obviously be impossible for him to arrive at an intelligent conclusion. It would be as ludicrous as attempting to discuss Plato without having read his Dialogues.

As a scientist and computer professional, I have examined the New Testament objectively and logically. It is my conclusion that these documents are indeed reliable historical records. We will then proceed, assuming that the information contained in the first four letters of the New Testament are a record of historical events. The evidence for the resurrection of Jesus Christ found in these letters will be placed into three categories: first, the physical and circumstantial evidence; second, the people who claimed they actually saw Jesus Christ alive after His death; and third, the people who opposed Christianity and yet were unable to disprove the resurrection.

PHYSICAL AND CIRCUMSTANTIAL EVIDENCES

As we begin this examination, we will first read two paragraphs from the book of John:

39   And Nicodemus came also, who had first come to Him by night; bringing a mixture of myrrh and aloes, about a hundred pounds weight.

40   And so they took the body of Jesus, and bound it in linen wrappings with the spices, as is the burial custom of the Jews.

41   Now in the place where He was crucified there was a garden; and in the garden a new tomb, in which no one had yet been laid.

42   Therefore on account of the Jewish day of preparation, because the tomb was nearby, they laid Jesus there.

—John 19

1   Now on the first day of the week Mary Magdalene came early to the tomb, while it was still dark, and saw the stone already taken away from the tomb.

2   And so she ran and came to Simon Peter, and to the other disciple whom Jesus loved, and said to them, "They have taken away the Lord out of the tomb, and we do not know where they have laid Him."

3   Peter therefore went forth, and the other disciple, and they were going to the tomb.

4   And the two were running together; and the other disciple ran ahead faster than Peter, and came to the tomb first;

5   and stooping and looking in, he saw the linen wrappings lying there; but he did not go in.

6   Simon Peter therefore also came, follow-

ing him, and entered the tomb; and he beheld
the linen wrappings lying there, . . .

—John 20

In this description of what transpired, it is
seen that the linen cloth that had wrapped Jesus'
body, which was interleaved with approximately 100
pounds of embalming paste and spices, remained in
the grave like an empty cocoon. Obviously, if the
body had been stolen, this "mummy-type" wrapping
would have been removed from the tomb with the
body.   Therefore, we will consider it one of our
first pieces of physical evidence.

However, the primary one is the empty tomb
itself.   No one has ever disputed the evidence of
the empty tomb.   Even in the first century, no one
claimed that the body was still there.   The Jews,
knowing the tomb was empty, devised a story to say
that the disciples had stolen the body.   The empty
tomb is an established, accepted fact.

Two additional pieces of physical evidence that
we will consider are the squad of policemen and the
stone which covered the entrance to the cave that
acted as the grave for Jesus Christ.   Again we will
have to call upon the New Testament for the
account:

> 62 Now on the next day, which is the one
> after the preparation, the chief priests and the
> Pharisees gathered together with Pilate,
> 63 and said, "Sir, we remember that when
> He was still alive that deceiver said, 'After
> three days I am to rise again.'
> 64 "Therefore, give orders for the grave to
> be made secure until the third day, lest the
> disciples come and steal Him away and say to
> the people, 'He has risen from the dead,' and
> the last deception will be worse than the
> first."

65 Pilate said to them, "You have a guard; go, make it as secure as you know how."

66 And they went and made the grave secure, and along with the guard they set a seal on the stone.

—Matthew 27

1 Now after the Sabbath, as it began to dawn toward the first day of the week, Mary Magdalene and the other Mary came to look at the grave.

2 And behold, a severe earthquake had occurred, for an angel of the Lord descended from heaven and came and rolled away the stone and sat upon it.

3 And his appearnace was like lightning, and his garment as white as snow;

4 and the guards shook for fear of him, and became like dead men.

5 And the angel answered and said to the women, "Do not be afraid; for I know that you are looking for Jesus who has been crucified.

6 "He is not here, for He has risen, just as He said. Come, see the place where He was lying.

7 "And go quickly and tell His disciples that He has risen from the dead; and behold, He is going before you into Galilee, there you will see Him; behold, I have told you."

8 And they departed quickly from the tomb with fear and great joy and ran to report it to His disciples.

9 And behold, Jesus met them and greeted them. And they came up and took hold of His feet and worshiped Him.

10 Then Jesus said to them, "Do not be afraid; go and take word to My brethren to leave for Galilee, and there they shall see Me."

11 Now while they were on their way, behold, some of the guard came into the city

and reported to the chief priests all that had happened.

12 And when they had assembled with the elders and counseled together, they gave a large sum of money to the soldiers,

13 and said, "You are to say, 'His disciples came by night and stole Him away while we were asleep.'

14 "And if this should come to the governor's ears, we will win him over and keep you out of trouble."

15 And they took the money and did as they had been instructed; and this story was widely spread among the Jews, and is to this day.

—Matthew 28

In this last reading, we see a squad of tough, riot-trained police sealing a huge rock covering the entrance to this cave.   They certainly would not have allowed a few frightened fishermen to steal the body from the tomb.   Obviously, the policemen would not have all gone to sleep on watch, since we all know the penalty for this, and indeed all of them would not have slept through a period when a group of groaning, sweating fishermen moved aside a stone probably weighing about two tons and removed a body from inside the cave.   Thus, in addition to the evidence of the empty tomb, we see the evidence of the moving of the stone, the breaking of the seal and the policemen on guard.

Since we have looked at the evidences that show that the tomb was indeed empty, then the question comes up "What happened to the body?" We will examine very briefly several possibilities.

1.   Christ never died at all.   This is not logical, since he was executed by professional executioners.

2. The enemies of Jesus Christ stole the body. This is also illogical, since His enemies were trying to disprove His resurrection. If they had stolen the body, all they would have had to do was produce it to disprove the resurrection and thus kill Christianity at its inception.

3. The disciples stole the body. This is very illogical, since all the disciples except John were executed or tortured to death, because of their faith in Jesus Christ. We can be sure this was real to them, for men will not die for a lie—particularly one of their own creation. These men were willing to die in order to proclaim that Jesus Christ arose from the dead.

4. Jesus Christ actually did rise from the dead. This is by far more logical than any of the other explanations.

In addition to the physical evidences of the empty tomb, the stone, the wrapping cloth, the soldiers and the broken seal, there is circumstantial evidence which would tend to further verify that the most logical explanation of the empty tomb is the resurrection of Jesus Christ.

The first circumstantial evidence that we would like to consider is the dramatic change in Christ's followers. Immediately after the crucifixion, they were whimpering, scared cowards. They were hiding in the upper room, fearful that someone might find them. Peter, the greatest of the disciples, denied ever having known Jesus Christ. Not only were they frightened, but some of them resumed their old occupation of commercial fishing. All of a sudden, seven weeks later, they stood in the middle of Jerusalem, boldly proclaiming that Jesus Christ had come back to life and 3,000 people became believers in a single day. How would you account for this change? The most logical explanationation is that they had actually seen Jesus Christ alive again and were convinced of His power.

Another circumstantial proof is the change of the "day of worship" from the Sabbath (Saturday) to the anniversary of the resurrection of Jesus Christ (Sunday). Since these Jewish men, reared in the traditions of Judaism, had been taught all their lives that Saturday was the day that God wanted them to rest and worship, something drastic must have happened in order for them to go against their years of religious training and practice. They felt that the resurrection of Jesus Christ was such a significant event in history that it should be commemorated weekly. To this day, we continue to celebrate the resurrection of Jesus Christ when we do not work on Sunday. This is the only historical event which we celebrate fifty-two times each year. Again, the most rational explanation for this change in the day of worship by the disciples is that they indeed saw Christ alive. Otherwise, they would not have had anything to celebrate on Sunday.

Since the people who saw Christ alive again after His execution are becoming a significant portion of the evidence we are examining, let's turn our attention directly to them.

THE PEOPLE WHO CLAIMED TO HAVE SEEN THE RISEN CHRIST

Let's first look at a summary of these people from a letter Paul wrote to believers in the city of Corinth:

> 3 For I delivered to you as of first importance what I also received, that Christ died for our sins according to the Scriptures,
> 4 and that He was buried, and that He

was raised on the third day according to the
Scriptures,
5 and that He appeared to Cephas, then to
the twelve.
6 After that He appeared to more than
five hundred brethren at one time, most of
whom remain until now, but some have fallen
asleep;
7 then He appeared to James, then to all
the apostles; . . .

—1 Corinthians 15

This states that more than 500 people saw
Jesus Christ alive after His death and burial. If we
were in the courtroom and had each of these 500
people testify for six minutes each, there would be
fifty hours of solid testimony. No court in the
world today would deny the occurrence of an event
with such overwhelming eye-witness evidence. The
possibility that 500 people could be hypnotized en
masse or could mass hallucinate is not even worth
considering, as any student of psychology will tell
you.

We would like to single out two of these 500
for special attention. It occurred this way, as recorded in the document by John:

24 But Thomas, one of the twelve, called
Didymus, was not with them when Jesus came.
25 The other disciples therefore were saying to him, "We have seen the Lord!" But he
said to them, "Unless I shall see in His hands
the imprint of the nails, and put my finger
into the place of the nails, and put my hand
into His side, I will not believe."
26 And after eight days again His disciples
were inside, and Thomas with them. Jesus
came, the doors having been shut, and stood in
their midst, and said, "Peace be with you."

27 Then He said to Thomas, "Reach here your finger, and see My hands; and reach here your hand, and put it into My side; and be not unbelieving, but believing."
28 Thomas answered and said to Him, "My Lord and my God!"
29 Jesus said to him, "Because you have seen Me, have you believed? Blessed are they who did not see, and yet believed."

—John 20

We see that John describes Thomas as being full of doubt, then becoming a devoted believer upon seeing Christ. If Thomas were to testify in a courtroom today, he would boldly testify, "I saw Him alive."

The other individual we would like to examine is Peter, the cocky, self-confident fisherman, who claimed that he would never deny Jesus Christ and yet who found himself even using profanity to emphasize the fact that he had never known Him. After the execution of his leader, Peter completely gave up hope and returned to his fishing occupation. Subsequent to this, Peter encountered the risen Christ, which was to begin an interesting transformation in his life:

1 After these things Jesus manifested Himself again to the disciples at the Sea of Tiberias, and He manifested Himself in this way.
2 There were together Simon Peter, and Thomas called Didymus, and Nathanael of Cana in Galilee, and the sons of Zebedee, and two others of His disciples.
3 Simon Peter said to them, "I am going fishing." They said to him, "We will also come with you." They went out and got into the boat; and that night they caught nothing.

4 But when the day was now breaking, Jesus stood on the beach; yet the disciples did not know that it was Jesus.

5 Jesus therefore said to them, "Children, you do not have any fish, do you?" They answered Him, "No."

6 And He said to them, "Cast the net on the right-hand side of the boat, and you will find a catch." They cast therefore, and then they were not able to haul it in because of the great number of fish.

7 That disciple therefore whom Jesus loved said to Peter, "It is the Lord." And so when Simon Peter heard that it was the Lord, he put his outer garment on (for he was stripped for work), and threw himself into the sea.

8 But the other disciples came in the little boat, for they were not far from the land, but about one hundred yards away, dragging the net full of fish.

9 And so when they got out upon the land, they saw a charcoal fire already laid, and fish placed on it, and bread.

10 Jesus said to them, "Bring some of the fish which you have now caught."

11 Simon Peter went up, and drew the net to land, full of large fish, a hundred and fifty-three; and although there were so many, the net was not torn.

12 Jesus said to them, "Come and have breakfast." None of the disciples ventured to question Him, "Who are You?" knowing that it was the Lord.

13 Jesus came and took the bread, and gave them, and the fish likewise.

14 This is now the third time that Jesus was manifested to the disciples, after He was raised from the dead.

15 So when they had finished breakfast, Jesus said to Simon Peter, "Simon, son of

John, do you love Me more than these?" He
said to Him, "Yes, Lord; You know that I love
You." He said to him, "Tend My lambs."

—John 21

Subsequently, we find that Peter was able to
preach with a boldness which is unparalleled. He
was executed eventually, because of his belief in
Jesus Christ and in the fact that Christ had risen
from the grave.

Lest the reader of this work assume that we
are only examining the evidences for and not
against the resurrection, let's now turn our
attention to those people who opposed Christ.

THE OPPONENTS OF CHRIST

The opponents of Jesus Christ fall into two
categories. The Jewish religious leaders were
against Christ for. the same reason that they had
had Him executed. He was a threat to their posi-
tiontion, power and religious beliefs. The Roman
officials were also opponents of Christianity, since
it was causing turmoil in one of their conquered
provinces.

Both of these groups tried to disprove the
resurrection and were unable to do so. If either
had stolen the body, they would have simply
produced it when the disciples proclaimed that He
had risen from the dead. The real leaders of
Judaism were so disturbed that they had Peter
arrested twice. They were willing to do anything
they could to kill this new movement. Yet, they
were unable to produce anything that could prove
that Christ had not risen from the dead.

CONCLUSION

Let's first summarize the evidences for the
resurrection of Jesus Christ from the dead:

1. *The physical evidence:*   There was the empty tomb; the policemen who were on hand, by order of the Council, to guard the body; and the seal which had been placed across the stone.   We also examined the stone itself and the cloth wrapping, which weighed over 100 pounds and yet remained in the cave that was the grave.

2. *The many people who claimed to have seen Christ alive after His execution:* There were 500 people who saw Jesus Christ after He came to life again.   Peter and Thomas were singled out for special attention, since there is recorded such a drastic change in each of them.

3. *The opponents of Christ:*   The early opponents tried very hard to disprove the resurrection.   Had there been a way in which they could have produced the body or otherwise disproved the resurrection, they certainly would have done so.

After examining the evidence, the most logical explanation for the empty tomb and the people who claimed that they saw Him, many of whom were willing to be executed for their belief, is that Jesus Christ came back to life after being executed, as He had predicted He would.   By doing so, He proved that He was God, that the claims He made while here on earth were indeed truth, and that He was able to fulfill all of His promises and commitments.

Most people today would like to have an internal peace and a fresh start in life.   Christ, God come to earth, said this:

27 "Peace I leave with you; My peace I give to you; not as the world gives, do I give to

you.   Let not your heart be troubled, nor let
it be fearful. . . ."

—John 14

Jesus Christ states here that He is leaving
with us His peace, if we believe in Him. He made
this statement a few days before He was executed.
Therefore, it would have to be the kind of peace
which will remain with us in spite of difficult
external circumstances. As St. Augustine once said:

Thou has made us for thyself, Oh
God, and our hearts are restless
until they find their rest in Thee.

Christ also stated that He is able to give us
a new start in life. Here again we turn to a
sentence in Paul's writing:

17 Therefore if anyone is in Christ, he is a
new creation; old things have passed away;
behold, all things have become new.

—2 Corinthians 5

The exciting promise of the New Testament is
that, just as Jesus Christ was resurrected, so will
be all those who believe in Him:

14 Now God has not only raised the Lord,
but will also raise us up through His power.

—1 Corinthians 6

In addition to promising that believers will
spend eternity in heaven with God (rather than
away from Him and His light and truth), Jesus
Christ makes other promises of what He will do for
us while we are yet alive and remain on this earth.
By believing in Him, as God, and allowing Him to
control our life and forgive our sins, He promises
to give us a new peace, a new power, a new

purpose in life and, indeed, a new heart. Since He made us and loves us very much, even enough to die for us, He will surely give us a happy, abundant life, if we allow Him to direct our course.

The Bible clearly claims that Jesus Christ rose from the dead. This is possibly *the* most important subject to examine, in our discussion of interesting subjects in the Bible. Because the Scriptures claim that Jesus was resurrected, and thus proved Himself to be the only begotten Son of God, it brings us head on to the question of who Jesus is. Who do you think Jesus Christ is? Do you think He rose from the dead? If He did, He is God, so why not commit your life to Him and begin to live this abundant, overflowing, yet peaceful life?

27

THE DANCE GOES ON

As you will see later, this chapter is really not about dancing. However, we will being by briefly mentioning the subject of dancing. There is nothing in the Bible that says we should not dance. In fact, progressively more churches are recognizing and using the dance as a form of worship. The Bible actually encourages the use of dance as a form of worship:

3 **Let them praise His name with dancing;**
Let them sing praises to Him
with timbrel and lyre.

—Psalm 149

4 **Praise Him with timbrel and dancing;**
Praise Him with stringed instruments
and pipe.

—Psalm 150

13 **"Then the virgin shall rejoice in the**
dance,
And the young men and the old,
together,
For I will turn their mourning into joy,
And will comfort them, and give them
joy for their sorrow. . . . "

—Jeremiah 31

Even King David—a man after God's own heart (Acts 13:22)—danced before the Lord, as an expression of his rejoicing:

14 And David was dancing before the Lord with all his might, and David was wearing a linen ephod.

—2 Samuel 6

About the only time that Jesus mentioned dancing, He certainly did not have any words of condemnation for it:

30 But the Pharisees and the lawyers rejected God's purpose for themselves, not having been baptized by John.
31 "To what then shall I compare the men of this generation, and what are they like?
32 "They are like children who sit in the market place and call to one another; and they say, 'We played the flute for you, and you did not dance; we sang a dirge, and you did not weep.'
33 "For John the Baptist has come eating no bread and drinking no wine; and you say, 'He has a demon!'
34 "The Son of Man has come eating and drinking and you say, 'Behold, a gluttonous man, and a drunkard, a friend of tax-gatherers and sinners!' . . ."

—Luke 7

The other occasion when Christ mentioned dancing was in connection with the return of the prodigal son. When the elder son came in from the field, he heard the music and saw the dancing and rejoicing for the wayward son who had come home:

22 "But the father said to his slaves, 'Quickly bring out the best robe and put it on

him, and put a ring on his hand and sandals
on his feet;
23 and bring the fattened calf, kill it, and
let us eat and be merry;
24 for this son of mine was dead, and has
come to life again; he was lost, and has been
found.' And they began to be merry.
25 "Now his older son was in the field,
and when he came and approached the house,
he heard music and dancing. . . ."

—Luke 15

If you take the overall teaching in the Bible
on dancing, it is obviously something that should
not be used in a lustful way, because lust is sin.
However, it can be used in a wholesome way for
rejoicing, celebrating at a feast or in worshiping
the Lord.

WORSHIPING A GOD WHO DOESN'T EXIST

As we have come to the concluding chapter in
this book, we need to reflect back over the book to
discern what its message truly is. In essence, this
book is really saying that many Christians—especially in America—are serving and worshiping a god
who does not exist. Their view of God might
include many of the following characteristics.

He would be against war
He would be against violence
He would never command someone to murder
    another
He would never make anyone sick
He would never bring drought and cause people
    to starve
He would never cause blindness or deafness
He would not allow His people to suffer
He would show mercy and love, even to
    constantly rebellious people

He would oppose nudity
He would be against multiple wives
He would condemn the practice of having permanent mistresses
He would not create dragons and unicorns
He would not have us worship Him at each new moon
He would be against wine and strong drink
He would be tolerant of other religions

As we have seen in this book, every one of these beliefs about God would be false, according to the Bible. What we are really saying is that the image of God that many Christians have does not really depict the God of the Bible, but a God that they have created to be the way they would like Him to be or think that He *should* be. But, remember, God does not change. He is the same yesterday, today and forever (Hebrews 13:8). The things that He did and approved of in the Old Testament are still part of His character and personality today.

It is time for the body of Christ—the true believers in Jesus Christ—to come back and find out who the God of the Bible really is, what He is like and then worship that God rather than the current one they worship, which is one of their own creation. If you are worshiping the god described in the preceding list, you are worshiping a false god—a god who does not exist. This book should be a clear call to all true believers to abandon any false image of God and worship the real God of the Bible.

THIS IS NOT THE END
IT IS REALLY JUST THE BEGINNING

There are so many things that could have been included in this book. Perhaps a second volume will be forthcoming, revealing what the Bible actually says about such subjects as the following:

Things God cannot do
Involvement in social issues
Political action
Civil disobedience by Christians
Christians in politics
Welfare
Can you talk to God and hear from God?
What we should eat
What food combinations we should have
Are Christians to obey the ten
    commandments?
"Cleaning up" the Bible
It is okay to have enemies
Cursing
Did Jesus have brothers; is Mary still a virgin?
How to pronounce a blessing
Angels—fact or fantasy?
Satan and hell—are they real?
The end of the age
The end of the world
Divine protection
Slavery
Rainbows and burning incense
The gospel according to Jesus
Is Jesus the only way to God?

The list could go on and on of interesting and exciting topics in the Bible. Many are things that a lot of people have no idea are in the Bible—subjects that many pastors, priests and rabbis would just as soon ignore. Yet God put these things in the Bible for a purpose.

I hope that you will not think of this as the end of a book, but just the beginning of an exciting time in your life when you personally are going to make some discoveries about what the greatest book in the world has to say. The Bible is very relevant to you and your life today and to the problems of society. It holds the answer to life, if we will just read it and heed it.

Of course, I believe the real answer to life and its problems is Jesus Christ. As we receive Him as our Savior and our Master, and we truly become His disciple and are filled with His Holy Spirit, we are going to have an abundant, rich and fulfilling life. Jesus Himself said, "I came that they might have life, and might have it abundantly" (John 10:10b).

Are you living life with a *capital* "L," full of joy, excitement and adventure? If not, you can have that abundant life, as you believe in Jesus Christ. If you have never made Him your Lord and Savior, I would encourage you to read Appendix A, which shares with you how to do this.

May God richly bless you as you discover afresh forgotten things in the most exciting book ever written, the Bible.

APPENDIX A

HOW TO BECOME A CHRISTIAN

If you are reading this, I am assuming that you are not sure that you have received Jesus Christ as your personal Savior. Not only is it possible to know this for sure, but God *wants* you to know. The following is what 1 John 5 has to say:

> **11 And the witness is this, that God has given us eternal life, and this life is in His Son.**
> **12 He who has the Son has the life; he who does not have the Son does not have the life.**
> **13 These things I have written to you who believe in the name of the Son of God, in order that you may know that you have eternal life.**

These things are written to us who believe in the name of the Son of God, so that we can know that we have eternal life. It is not a "guess so," or "hope so" or "maybe so" situation. It is so that we can know for certain that we have eternal ife. If you do not have this confidence, please read on.

In order to get to the point of knowing that we have eternal life, we need to first go back and review some basic principles. First, it is important to note that all things that God created (the stars, trees, animals, and so on) are doing exactly what they were created to do, except man. Isaiah indicates why God created us:

> 7 ". . . Everyone who is called by My
>   name,
>   And whom I have created for My glory,
>   Whom I have formed even whom I have
>   made."
>
> —Isaiah 3

This says that humans were created to glorify God. I am sure that neither you nor I have glorified God all of our lives in everything that we have done. This gives us our first clue as to what "sin" is. We find more about it in Romans 3:

> 23 for all have sinned and fall short of the glory of God . . .

This says that we have all sinned and that we all fall short of the purpose for which we were created—that of glorifying God. I have an even simpler definition of sin. I believe that sin is "living independent of God." A young person out of high school can choose which college to attend. If he makes this decision apart from God, it is "sin." This was the basic problem in the garden of Eden. Satan tempted Eve to eat the fruit of the tree of the "knowledge of good and evil." He said that if she would do this, she would know good from evil and would be wise like God. This would mean that she could make her own decisions and would not have to rely on God's wisdom and guidance. Since you and I fit in the category of living independent of God and not glorifying Him in everything we do, we need to look at what the results of this sin are.

First let me ask you what "wages" are. After thinking about it, because you probably receive wages from your job, you will probably come up with a definition something like "wages are what you get paid for what you do." That is a good answer. Now let's see what the Bible has to say concerning his:

> **23 For the wages of sin is death, but the free gift of God is eternal life in Christ Jesus our Lord.**
>
> **—Romans 6**

Here we see that the wages of sin is death—spiritual, eternal death. Death is what we get paid for the sin that we do. Yet this passage also gives us the other side of the coin: that is, that through Jesus Christ we can freely have eternal life, instead of eternal death. Isn't that wonderful!

But let's return for a moment to this death penalty that the people without Christ have hanging over their heads, because of the sin that they live in. In the Old Testament, God made a rule: "The soul who sins will die" (Ezekiel 18:4). If we were able to live a perfect, sinless life, we could make it to heaven on our own. If we live anything less than a perfect life, according to God's rule, we will not make it to heaven, but instead will be sentenced to death. All through the Bible we find no one living a good enough life to make it to heaven.

This brings us to the place where Jesus Christ fits into this whole picture. His place was beautifully illustrated to me when I was considering receiving Christ as my Savior, by a story about a judge in a small town.

In this small town, the newspapermen were against the judge and wanted to get him out of office. A case was coming up before the judge concerning a vagrant—a drunken bum—who happened to have been a fraternity brother of the judge when they were at college. The newspapermen thought that this was their chance. If the judge let the vagrant off easy, the headlines would read, "Judge Shows Favoritism to Old Fraternity Brother." If the judge gave the vagrant the maximum penalty, the headlines would read, "Hardhearted Judge Shows No Mercy to Old Fraternity Brother." Either way they had him. The judge heard the case and gave the vagrant the maximum penalty of thirty days or $300 fine.

The judge then stood up, took off his robe, laid it down on his chair, walked down in front of the bench and put his arm around the shoulders of his old fraternity brother. He told him that as judge, in order to uphold the law, he had to give him the maximum penalty, because he was guilty. But because he cared about him, he wanted to pay the fine for him. So the judge took out his wallet and handed his old fraternity brother $300.

For God to be "just," He has to uphold the law that says "the soul who sins will die." On the other hand, because He loves us He wants to pay that death penalty for us. I cannot pay the death penalty for you because I have a death penalty of my own that I have to worry about, since I, too, have sinned. If I were sinless, I could die in your place. I guess God could have sent down millions of sinless beings to die for us. But what God chose to do was to send down *one* Person, who was equal in value, in God's eyes, to all of the people who will ever live, and yet who would remain sinless. Jesus Christ died physically and spiritually in order to pay the death penalty for you and me. The blood of Christ washes away all of our sins, and with it the death penalty that resulted from our sin.

The judge's old fraternity brother could have taken the $300 and said thank you, or he could have told the judge to keep his money and that he would do it on his own. Similarly, each person can thank God for allowing Christ to die in his place and receive Christ as his own Savior, or he can tell God to keep His payment and that he will make it on his own.   What you do with that question determines where you will spend eternity.

Referring to Christ, John 1 says this:

> 12 But as many as received Him, to them He gave the right to become children of God, even to those who believe in His name . . .

John 3:16 says:

> 16 "For God so loved the world, that He gave His only begotten Son, that whoever believes in Him should not perish but have eternal life. . . ."

Here we see that if we believe in Christ we won't perish, but we will have everlasting life and the right to become children of God.   Right now you can tell God that you believe in Christ as the Son of God, that you are sorry for your sins and that you want to turn from them.   You can tell Him that you want to accept Christ's payment for your sins, and yield your life to be controlled by Christ and the Holy Spirit.   (You must accept Christ as your Savior *and your MASTER*.)

If you pray such a prayer, Christ will come and dwell within your heart and you will know for sure that you have eternal life.

If you have any questions about what you have just read, I would encourage you to go to someone that you know, who really knows Jesus Christ as his Savior, and ask him for help and guidance. After you receive Christ, I would encourage you to become a part of a group of believers in Christ who study the Scriptures together, worship God together and have a real love relationship with each other. This group (body of believers) can help nurture you and build you up in your new faith in Jesus Christ.

If you have received Christ as a result of reading these pages, I would love to hear from you. My address is at the end of this book.

Welcome to the family of God.

James McKeever

APPENDIX B

MEET THE AUTHOR

Dr. James McKeever is an international consulting economist, lecturer, author, world traveler, and Bible teacher. His financial consultations are utilized by scores of individuals from all over the world who seek his advice on investment strategy and international affairs.

Dr. McKeever is the editor and major contributing writer of the *McKeever Strategy Letter*, an economic and investment letter with worldwide circulation and recognition, rated #1 for 1985 and 1986 by an independent newsletter-rating service, and showing an average profit of 59.6 percent per year over the last ten years (1978-1987). He is also editor of the *Mutual Fund Advantage* newsletter, which helps the smaller investor profit from the increasingly-popular area of mutual funds. ·

Dr. McKeever has been a featured speaker at monetary, gold and tax haven conferences in London, Zurich, Bermuda, Amsterdam, South Africa, Australia, Singapore and Hong Kong, as well as all over the North American continent and Latin America.

As an economist and futurist, Dr. McKeever has shared the platform with such men as Ronald Reagan, Gerald Ford, William Simon, William Buckley, Alan Greenspan, heads of foreign governments, and many other outstanding thinkers.

For five years after completing his academic work, Dr. McKeever was with a consulting firm which specialized in financial investments in petroleum. Those who were following his counsel back in 1954 invested heavily in oil.

For more than ten years he was with IBM, where he held several key management positions. During those years, when IBM was just moving into transistorized computers, he helped that company become what it is today. With IBM, he consulted with top executives of many major corporations in America, helping them solve financial, control and information problems. He has received many awards from IBM, including the "Key Man Award" and the "Outstanding Contribution Award." He is widely known in the computer field for his books and articles on management, management control and information sciences.

In addition to this outstanding business background, Dr. McKeever is an ordained minister. He has been a Baptist evangelist, pastor of Catalina Bible Church for three and a half years (while still with IBM) and a frequent speaker at Christian conferences. He has the gift of teaching and an indepth knowledge of the Bible, and has authored ten best-selling Christian books, five of which have won the "Angel Award."

Dr. McKeever is president of Omega Ministries, which is a nonprofit organization established under the leading of the Holy Spirit to minister to the body of Christ by the traveling ministry of anointed men of God, through books, cassettes, seminars, conferences, and video tapes. He is the editor of the widely-read newsletter, *End-Times News Digest* (published by Omega Ministries), which relates the significance of current events to biblical prophecy and to the body of Christ today. The worldwide outreach of Omega Ministries is supported by the gifts of those who are interested.

DETAILED OUTLINE

294

THE
VICTORY
BIBLE
READING
PLAN

It's new! It's exciting!

You will read the Bible not in the regular old way
but in the sequence in which things actually
happened. You will love it! START ANYTIME! (over)

VICTORY BIBLE READING PLAN

Perhaps this book has inspired you to read through the Bible for
yourself. We certainly hope so. This popular Bible reading guide can help
you do so.

Many people have tried various plans for reading through the Bible
in a year and have found that they tend to get bogged down. The Lord
woke James McKeever at 2 a.m. one morning and gave him an exciting
new way of reading through the Bible. It has three unique characteristics:

1. You read a Psalm or a Proverb each day.
2. You read the gospels twice.
3. You read the Old Testament in chronological sequence.

There are many exciting features about *The Victory Bible Reading Plan*. One is that you read a Psalm or a chapter of Proverbs every day, which brings a refreshment to your daily Bible reading.

When Christians have been polled, it has been found that 85 percent of them concentrate more on the epistles than the gospels. If we are going to try to become like Jesus Christ, we need to keep an image of Him fresh before our eyes. In this plan, you go through the four gospels twice during the year, but not one after the other, as in most Bible reading plans. For example, you read Matthew, then Acts, Mark, then Romans, Luke, then first and second Corinthians and so forth.

One very exciting thing is that you read the Old Testament, not in the sequence that the books are found in the Bible, but in the sequence in which the events occurred. For example, Daniel and Ezekiel wrote during the Babylonian captivity, and Ezra came back from that captivity to rebuild the temple. Therefore, you read them in that sequence. Also, while reading 1 Kings, when Solomon becomes king, you branch off and read Song of Solomon and Ecclesiastes. While reading 2 Kings, when Jonah becomes a prophet, you go over and read the book of Jonah.

You will find that the Old Testament will come alive, as these books are placed in their proper chronological sequence. Try it—you'll love it.

Start anytime, and a year later you will have read through the entire Bible! God will change you through it, as He has thousands of others.

Many churches use this for their entire congregation. As they, as a group, have begun to daily let God speak to them through the Scriptures, pastors have commented that the entire spiritual level of the church has risen. There are significant discounts available for volume orders.

> 1-9 copies . . . . . . $1.00 each
> 10-99 copies. . . . . . $ .50 each
> 100-199 copies . . . . . $ .45 each
> 200 or more copies. . . $ .40 each

(You may use the convenient order form on the last page to order this.)

298

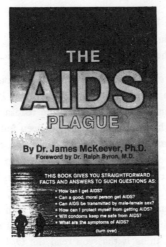

TO THE AUTHOR

Some of the materials available from Dr. McKeever are shown in summary on the reverse side. Please indicate your area of interest, remove this page and mail it to Omega Publications.

Dr. McKeever would appreciate hearing any personal thoughts from you. If you wish to comment, write your remarks below on this reply form.

Comments:

ORDER FORM

Omega Publications
P.O. Box 4130
Medford, OR 97501

$_____ Please send me _____ copies of your
popular *Victory Bible Reading Plan* ($1)

Please send me the following books by
Dr. McKeever:
(Prices subject to change without notice)

Qty

___ $_____ *The AIDS Plague* (Revised and
Expanded—$6.95)
___ _____ *Financial Guidance* ($7.95)
___ _____ *You Can Overcome* ($6.95)
___ _____ *Become Like Jesus* ($6.95)
___ _____ *The Rapture Book* ($6.95)
___ _____ *The Coming Climax of History*
($6.95)
___ _____ *Revelation for Laymen* ($5.95)
___ _____ *It's in the Bible* (Hardback—$19.95)

Please send me more information about:

☐ Dr. McKeever speaking at our church or
Christian conference
☐ Cassette tapes
☐ Video tapes

Please send the materials I have indicated to:

Name_____

Address_____

City, State_____Zip_____